MW00814024

FRITZ VON ERICH:

Master of the Iron Claw

REVISED EDITION

Ron G. Mullinax

FRITZ VON ERICH: Master of the Iron Claw
(REVISED EDITION)

Copyright © 2017 by **Ron G. Mullinax.**

Library of Congress Control Number:		2016950998
ISBN: 13	Paperback	978-1-63524-981-1
	PDF	978-1-63524-982-8
	ePub	978-1-63524-983-5
	Kindle	978-1-63524-984-2
	Hardcover	978-1-63524-993-4

All rights reserved. No part of this book may be reproduced or transmitted in any form or by any means, electronic or mechanical, including photocopying, recording, or by any information storage and retrieval system, without permission in writing from the copyright owner.

Printed in the United States of America.

LitFire LLC
1-800-511-9787
www.litfirepublishing.com
order@litfirepublishing.com

DEDICATION

I would like to dedicate this book to my mother and father (Bill and Sue Mullinax); my son, Shaun Ray Mullinax; my editor, Naomi Crouch; and a special thanks to my friends Kendall Cook and Richard Lack for all the help, inspiration, and support they gave me in putting together this history of a great man and the legacy he left behind. In addition, my thanks to all the Von Erich fans around the world.

—Ron Mullinax

INTRODUCTION

In late June 1997, Jack Adkisson, better known to older wrestling fans around the world as Fritz Von Erich, "The Master of the Iron Claw," was diagnosed with terminal brain cancer at Baylor Medical Center in Dallas, Texas.

To help Fritz through his painful last months, I moved into his home on Lake Dallas in Denton County, Texas. In the months that followed, Jack Adkisson and I became the closest of friends. I did my best to take care of him and make his final days as pleasant as possible until he passed away in September of that year. I would not accept compensation from the Adkisson family for the help I gave Fritz through his illness. In fact, I considered it a privilege to spend those last few months with a man I have always considered my life-long hero. Being by his side as he passed from this world was an experience that has touched my life in so many ways.

Growing up in Wichita Falls, Texas, my parents were immense wrestling fans. Professional wrestling became a big part of my life at a very early age. I can remember my sister and I looking forward to Thursday nights, when our family would pile in our old green Chevy pick-up truck and head out to the local wrestling matches.

On Saturday mornings, I would sit in front of the television set watching NWA Championship Wrestling. It was there that I saw Fritz Von Erich for the very first time, using his patented "Iron Claw." Fritz was wrestling Gene Kiniski, an ex-world champion from Canada who used another version of the claw, referred to as the "Abdominal Claw." Kiniski also used another deadly wrestling hold that he claimed to be the master of, known as the "Sleeper Hold."

It was 1962 and I was 10 years old at the time. That wrestling match sticks in my mind as if it were yesterday. I will never forget seeing Fritz Von Erich that Saturday morning as he entered the ring dressed in black wrestling trunks with a bright red cape draped across his shoulders. A large, claw-like hand with long fingernails had been embroidered on the back of his cape. As Fritz entered the ring with a sneer on his face, he held his right arm high up in the air, grabbed his right wrist with his left hand, and began to turn slowly in a circle showing the fans his deadly, patented Iron Claw.

The upcoming match had been all the announcers and promoters could talk about in the past two weeks on Saturday morning NWA wrestling. This huge, six-foot-six, 275-pound German wrestler who claimed he hated all Americans was the talk of the wrestling world. The fans down south were to get their first look at who the wrestling promoters were calling the most feared man in professional wrestling. I remember talking my father into buying me the latest NWA wrestling magazine that was doing a feature story on Fritz with his picture on the front cover. Dad had agreed to buy me the magazine. He and I stopped at three different stores, but they had sold out within the first few days of putting them on the shelves. I had to count the days as I waited for that particular Saturday morning so I could judge for myself what was being said about this German wrestler and his feared Iron Claw.

What a wrestling match that turned out to be, with the two men battling to win two out of three falls. Fritz won the first fall after jumping off the second rope and catching Kiniski on the side of the head with a knee, knocking him out. The second fall was full of excitement, with both Gene and Fritz throwing each other out of the ring and beating one another over the head with the ringside metal chairs. Following a long struggle, Gene won the second fall after getting Fritz in the center of the ring and applying his sleeper hold.

As the third and final fall began, I found myself on the edge of my chair, screaming for Fritz to win. To this day, I am still not quite sure why I started cheering for Fritz Von Erich. Maybe it was the way he seemed to take total control of the match. About five minutes into the third round, he knocked Kiniski down to the mat. With a sneer on his face, Fritz dropped to his knees in the center of the ring and clamped a very large right hand around the top of Gene Kiniski's head.

I will never forget the look of agony on Kiniski's face as Fritz began to apply pressure to the upper part of the head. Blood had started trickling down the left side of Gene's face, and then the right side started bleeding as he screamed in pain. With arms waving wildly in the air, Gene managed to get to his feet as he tried every way to break the tremendous grip that was causing him so much agony. Blood had started to flow freely as it began to puddle on the mat. After what had to be over a minute under Fritz's claw-like grip, Gene began losing consciousness. As the blood supply was being cut off to the brain, Kiniski fell back to his knees on the ring apron. The referee, along with all the fans at ringside, stood with their mouths open, not believing what was taking place in front of their eyes. Fritz turned his head, looking for the referee, and screamed out something. After the referee woke up, he ran over to Kiniski, looked at his blood-soaked face, picked Gene's right arm up in the air, and let it drop. Gene's limp arm fell back to his side as the referee turned his head and screamed out, "Ring the bell! Ring the bell!" Fritz won the match that morning due to Kiniski not being able to continue the final round.

From that point on, I was a true Fritz Von Erich fan. I made a point of watching Fritz whenever one of his matches was on television. I devoured every wrestling magazine I could find bearing the name "Von Erich." Clipping and saving articles about his life and career was my favorite pastime.

In junior high school, during physical education class in Graford, Texas, I even used the Iron Claw myself during a fight with one of my classmates. The fight had started over an argument between the two of us. Which sport was better, wrestling or boxing? My classmate told me that Mohammad Ali could beat Fritz Von Erich's butt, then punched me in the mouth. As in most fights between two young men, we later found ourselves on the ground, wrestling.

After rolling around on the ground, I got lucky and wound up on top of my fellow classmate. It was then that I applied the Iron Claw to my challenger's head, digging my fingernails into the sides of his face just as Fritz would have done. The young student had a bad acne problem. My long fingernails busted some of the pimples open, making him bleed just enough to get me in big trouble with our basketball coach, who had watched the first few minutes of the fight. He broke it up after seeing blood. The two of us were sent to the principal's office that afternoon, where I got into more trouble because I could not explain the smile on my face. I was very proud of myself that day because I knew deep down that I had won my very first fight.

Little did I know that one day, I would not only meet my hero in person but also would sit by his side and hold his hand as he passed from this world.

A few years after that first Saturday-morning wrestling match, I learned that a dispute had arisen between Fritz and the National Wrestling Association's promoters in the New York and Canadian area where Fritz wrestled for so many years. Fritz made a public announcement on television that shocked fans throughout the nation. He told the public that his real name was Jack Adkisson and that he was really born and raised in Jewett, Texas—not Berlin, Germany, as the promoters had told all the fans and the press. He told all fans that due to a disagreement between the northern NWA promoters and himself, he was quitting wrestling and moving back home to Texas.

Shortly before 1966, Fritz did come home to Texas. In Dallas he started setting up his headquarters and establishing the organization that would become known as World Class Championship Wrestling.

I had been overjoyed to hear the news that the man I had come to admire so much was actually from my home state and did not really hate all Americans. After hearing that news, I became an even more avid Von Erich fan. Whenever Fritz was on the bill at the Southside Sportatorium in Dallas—or any other town that I could get to—I made sure to attend. Many years later, after doctors diagnosed Fritz with cancer, Gene Kiniski got word of Fritz's terminal illness and made a trip from Canada to spend a week with his longtime friend and adversary. I will remember that week for the rest of my life. Both Gene and Fritz reminisced daily about the good old days of professional wrestling while I took in every word they said, not quite believing I was in the same room with two of the greatest pro wrestlers in the history of the sport.

I first met Jack Adkisson after a mutual friend in Dallas introduced me to Kevin, Fritz's second-oldest and now only living son. The year was late 1993, just shortly after Fritz's fourth-oldest son, Kerry, had committed suicide. I had watched Kevin and his brothers wrestle for many years both on television and live at the Southside Sportatorium and Texas Stadium, where, on several occasions, Fritz and his sons' matches attracted more than 50,000 screaming fans.

Kevin and I found that we had a lot in common, being such big wrestling fans and me a big Von Erich fan. In addition, we both loved the outdoors. I had spent four years in the United States Marine Corps and had barely made it through a tour in Vietnam. Kevin had expressed an interest in knowing what it was like being a Marine in late 1960 and in the middle of a war no one wanted.

Kevin, his wife Pam, and their four children were living in Jefferson, Texas, when we first met. Kevin, who had all but retired from the ring, spent a lot of time driving to Denton to check up on his father. Fritz lived alone in a small, frame house on his 150-acre Lake Dallas ranch.

Kevin would come by my house in Irving, Texas, to wait for the traffic to let up before continuing on to Jefferson. We would drink a couple of beers and watch the Ultimate Fighting Challenge, boxing, wrestling, football, or hockey games. I would even record many sporting events for us to watch later when Kevin would drop by. Mostly, Kevin and I would talk about his father, brothers, and what a great life they had while growing up in a wrestling family and all the places he had traveled throughout the world. Kevin would give me the latest scoop on the current wrestlers, what they were like in real life and some of their greatest matches. I really enjoyed the times we spent together. Sometimes, after one too many beers, I would start to ask Kevin about various wrestling holds. He would always smile and say, "Here, let me show you." We would end up on the floor with Kevin making me holler "uncle." It did not take long for me to stop asking him to show me a wrestling hold.

A little over a year after Kevin and I met, he and his family moved to the Denton area to be near his father. Fritz was having more and more medical problems than ever before. That is when Kevin introduced me to my long-time hero, Fritz Von Erich.

When I first met Fritz I had been working in the personal computer field for many years. Fritz, who invested heavily in the stock market, asked if I would be interested in showing him how to use a personal computer to track his stocks in real time. I had recently undergone back surgery and was not working, so I jumped at the opportunity.

After each day's lessons were over and the stock markets had closed, Fritz would break out a bottle of Scotch. Over drinks, he would tell me about the old days of professional wrestling, about raising his six sons, and all the places around the world he had traveled during his 35-plus years in the wrestling business. In return, I talked about my experiences in the Marine Corps, my tour in Vietnam, and all the years I followed wrestling while I was growing up.

As we became the closest of friends, Fritz told me about all the tragedies he and his family had endured throughout the years; how he could not understand why he had lost five of his six sons and suffered through a divorce from his one true love, Doris Smith, after forty-two years of marriage.

Jack Adkisson was more than a great athlete and professional wrestler. He was a very wonderful and kind man as well. After the doctors diagnosed Fritz with terminal cancer, he gave me some irreplaceable photos and videos. When I would not accept any compensation for the help I gave him during his illness, he said, "Why don't you write a book about me, from me, to all my fans around the world like you, Ron, and let everyone hear the Von Erich story from me."

It sounded like a good idea, so I started the long process of taking notes the best I could, attempting to put down on paper all the wonderful stories that Fritz, Doris, and Kevin shared with me throughout the years of our friendship. To put together something that Fritz Von Erich himself would find worthy of his approval was the challenge.

CHAPTER 1

I will begin my story in 1996, when I had known the Adkisson family for a little more than two years. One morning, I received a phone call from Fritz asking if I would be interested in a job. Fritz wanted to learn to use a personal computer so he would be able to track his stocks and monitor the stock markets in real time. This request first came in the form of a challenge from Fritz. He explained to me over the phone that his ex-wife, Doris, had once tried to teach him about computers and MS/DOS. After a few days of doing the best he could, they had both become so confused that they soon gave up. In defense of Fritz and Doris, however, that was a few years before Microsoft made things much easier by introducing Windows 95 to the computer world.

I did my best to try to explain Windows to Fritz over the phone. I told him all he needed to know was how to move the mouse around the mouse pad, point at the subject he was interested in, and push a button. Fritz was not convinced he would be able to learn, saying, "That just sounds too damned easy." Nevertheless, he hired me to teach him anyway.

I cannot tell you how thrilled I was for the opportunity to work with a man I admired as much as the legendary Fritz Von Erich. Early the next morning, before my first day on the job, I sat down at my computer and logged on to the Internet. I began a search on the World Wide Web for everything I could find about the Von Erich family.

When I arrived at Fritz's house later that morning, we sat down at his dining room table and poured ourselves each a cup of coffee. I began to explain to him the best I could about the Internet. Then I showed him all the information I had printed out about him and his sons. Fritz soon became engrossed in reading about the exploits of the Von Erich wrestling dynasty he had created more than three decades ago. I asked Fritz if he would like to come back to my house and see my computer, telling him we could log on to the financial sites and get a better idea of what computers could accomplish. I could also show him all the different Von Erich sites that fans had put up in memory of the dynasty. Instead of my idea, Fritz had a better one. We went to the mall to buy him his own computer, his gateway to the online world.

Fritz turned out to be a very fast learner. His only problem was that he had a hard time moving the mouse around and clicking the buttons. The first three fingers on Fritz's right hand seemed to all bend in a different direction at the knuckle. When I asked about his fingers, he told me that most of the fingers on his right hand had been broken more times than he could remember. The first thing most opponents tried when attempting to break the Iron Claw was to grab the fingers. Then, they would bend the fingers backward, many times breaking them at the knuckle. Over many years, arthritis had settled into the joints of his fingers and knuckles. At times, he had trouble picking up the smallest of objects with his right hand. However, after a few days and a few adjustments, he seemed to master that mouse just as he had mastered most everything else he had ever tried to do in his life.

Every morning I would get up early and drive the thirty-five miles from my house in Irving to Fritz's house at Lake Dallas. We would start the day by reheating yesterday's coffee and going over any financial news that may have come in during the night.

Fritz had a very strange way of making what he called a "good pot of coffee." He would first put two large scoops of coffee in the coffee maker, add just a little salt to take care of the bitter taste, take half a pot of yesterday's coffee, fill the rest of the pot back up with tap water, and pour the concoction through the coffee maker. After a couple of cups of this ultra-strong brew, we would start bouncing off the walls so badly we would have to get up and go for our morning walk.

Fritz owned 150 prime acres on Lake Dallas, where he lived alone in an old, small, two-bedroom house after he and his wife divorced. Our walks were never very long. Not only had most of the fingers on Fritz's right hand been broken, but at one time or another most of the bones in the rest of his body had been broken as well. Fritz had undergone three knee surgeries on his right knee and two on his left knee. Throughout the years, he had also undergone two hip replacements, lumbar back surgery, and not to mention more concussions than he said he could remember. The arthritis in his lower joints was so bad he could hardly stand up, much less walk any distance. He also wore hearing aids in both ears due to the many times wrestling opponents had slapped him upside the head. Repeated blows throughout his life had damaged both eardrums, which accounted for the near total loss of hearing in both ears. His equilibrium had been severely damaged, causing balance problems as well. All these aches and pains were his payback for the many years of stepping in the ring and giving his fans their money's worth and more. For Fritz, every match was a war. Trust me when I say that I do not think you could find a wrestler who had ever climbed in the ring with Fritz Von Erich who would tell you any different.

In Fritz's early days of wrestling, he told me that he'd quickly learned that he had to be tough or he would not have made it in the wrestling business. "I would be in one city one night for a show and after it was over I would have to drive to another city and be ready for a match the next night. There was other times when I might wrestle two or three times in one day," Fritz said. "Even if I had been hurt in a match the night before, I had to be ready to fight again soon or the promoters would not book me for any more matches. I had to wrestle, or my family would go hungry. In addition, all this was for three dollars per match in those days. Sometimes that would not be enough money to cover my transportation costs and I would have to get an advance from the promoter to make it to the next match. You had to love the sport of wrestling to make it in those days." Fritz would say that he often wondered how he ever made it to sixty-eight years of age.

During our walk one morning, I asked Fritz if he took any type of medicine to help him through the pain. "Nothing," he said. "Well, maybe a couple of glasses of Scotch if the pain got really bad. After several years of waking up every morning feeling as if a train had ran over me, I guess a person just gets used to hurting in one place or another. Anyone who chooses a career in sports had better be able to cope with the daily aches and pains without reaching for a bottle of pills. Pain pills are something that you take when the pain is so bad that your body can no longer function without some type of relief. Too many good athletes have wrecked their career with pills. Best thing is just to learn to do without them."

After Fritz and I finished our little walks every morning, we always got back to the house in time to watch CNBC Market Watch and try to figure out what the stock markets would do that day.

I had never understood Wall Street—or the stock market, for that matter—until I met Fritz. The man had made nothing less than a fortune by putting to use his in-depth knowledge of the financial world. Day after day he explained the markets to me and I would try my best to explain computers and the Internet to him. My biggest problem with Fritz and the computer was that he could not understand that there is more than one way to do things in Windows 95. He would catch me doing something different than I had showed him previously and all hell would break loose. I was almost fifty years old when I met Fritz and had spent four years in the Marine Corps and a tour in 'Nam. After the service, I worked for a couple years as a Seattle police officer before returning to Texas. Very few people can shake me up;

however, at sixty-seven years old, Fritz could be as intimidating as any man I believe I have ever met. If he got mad and yelled at me, I would feel it all the way to the bone.

When he explained to me how the markets worked, I made sure to listen. Fritz had invested much of his own money in the markets and had been doing so since 1972, when a friend introduced him to a stock broker who guaranteed Fritz that he could double, even triples any investment. Fritz told me that he took the broker up on the deal and the guy more than quadrupled his investment the first year. "I was hooked after that," Fritz said. "I started urging all my friends and family members to do the same."

Fritz was very generous with his knowledge, frequently giving advice on what stocks and funds to buy, when to buy them, and when to get out of them. Everyone who took his advice did very well in the markets.

The first sign that Fritz was ill came at the end of June 1997, after I had been working at Fritz's house almost daily for about eight months.

Normally, when I arrived at Fritz's home, he would be awake and watching the early morning news. However, on this particular morning I walked in the door to find him sitting at his kitchen table with his head down. The TV was off and the coffee had not been made. Alarmed, I sat down next to him and called his name. It was not until I repeated his name a second time that he looked up and became aware of me sitting there at the kitchen table with him.

The first words out of his mouth were, "Ron, something's wrong with me. I feel strange inside." I asked him what he meant by "strange," but he said he could not explain it. "All I know is that something's wrong," he said, in a very weak voice.

I asked Fritz if he wanted me to take him to the hospital. He declined. He just wanted to rest and insisted I should go back home and call him the next day. I told him that I was very worried about him and did not want to leave him alone if he was not feeling well. Especially since his son Kevin was in Costa Rica on a two-week family vacation.

He urged me not to worry, saying Kevin would be back the following day and that if he did not feel better by then, he would have Kevin take him to the doctor. "You have earned a few days off, Ron, go out and try to have some fun for a change." He promised to call if he started feeling worse and needed my help.

I followed Fritz's advice and went on home that day, only to spend my time sitting around the house and worrying about my new friend. When I called that evening to check on him, he said he was feeling better and was planning to pick Kevin and his family up at the airport first thing in the morning.

The next morning, I called again to find out how he was feeling. I thought that I would offer to pick up Kevin and his family at DFW airport if he was still feeling bad. Fritz said he was okay and that he was on his way out the door and headed for the airport. He sounded like his old self again, so I told him I was going to drive to Athens, Texas, to see my parents and would be back in couple of days. I said I would call when I got back so we could continue our computer lessons. I drove to my parents' house and spent the day with them, but decided to return to Irving late that night because of a bad feeling that I had all day.

I am glad I drove back home that night, because very early the next morning came a knock at the door. I opened the door and found Kevin standing there looking horrible. Kevin came in and sat down in a chair and began to fill me in on what was going on with his dad.

"After Dad picked up the family at the airport, we started back to Denton," Kevin said. "Dad started feeling bad and had to pull over to the side of the road and let me drive. As we were getting out of the truck to change places, Dad got halfway around the truck, stopped, grabbed the top of his head, and fell to one knee. He was lucky that he was able to grab the side of the truck with his free hand or he would have fallen on his face. I told him that I was going to take him to Baylor Medical Center in Dallas, but he made me take Pam and the kids home first. Later, after we got to Baylor, the doctors admitted him for observation and tests. Dad said he just felt like something was not right with him," Kevin said. "Dad knows his body very well; if he says something's not right, I believe him. I have never seen him act like this before. I am starting to think something bad is wrong with him."

Later that day, I visited Fritz in the hospital. He was making jokes and flirting with all the nurses, saying he could not wait to get home and start working on the computer again. He asked if I would track his stocks for him and let him know what was happening on Wall Street. I promised to print a copy of his portfolio and bring it with me the next time I came to see him.

A few days later the upbeat mood was shattered when the test results came in. That is when Kevin and his family learned that the doctors had found a tumor in Fritz's head and that cancer was spreading through the rest of his body. The doctors explained to Kevin that the cancer was well into the advanced stages. "There is not much that can be done to treat the cancer at this late stage. If he starts chemotherapy immediately, he might have six months left to live—if he is very lucky," the doctor said.

Fritz stayed at Baylor for about two weeks before he was able to go back to his house on Lake Dallas. While Fritz was in the hospital, Kevin stopped by my house in Irving one day and told me he had worked out a plan to try to get his mother and father back together before it was too late.

He had called his mother—who had moved to Vicksburg, Mississippi, shortly after she and Fritz had gotten a divorce— and told her the bad news that Dad was dying. "He would like to see you one more time before it is too late," Kevin told his mother. Then, Kevin went back to Baylor Hospital, where he told his father that Mom had heard the news on TV and called to see how he was feeling and wanted to come and see him, if he would allow it. Fritz had agreed, and so Kevin's plan had worked. His mother was going to make that long drive from Vicksburg, Mississippi to be with the man who had always been there for her in her time of need.

I first met Doris Smith, Fritz's ex-wife, in 1994, a few months before I met Fritz. After their divorce, Doris had moved to a rather large three-story Southern home in Vicksburg. The house was well built and looked new, even though it had been completed back in 1903. Doris had a large garden in the back of the house and spent most of her days pulling weeds, working around the house, and generally trying to keep herself occupied.

Doris and Fritz had divorced in 1993, just a few short months before their fourth-oldest son, Kerry, had committed suicide. Doris was an attractive woman who looked much younger than her years. She certainly did not look like a mother who had lost five children in her lifetime. I had met Doris after Kevin called one day to say he was going to go to Vicksburg to visit his mother. "Want to ride along?" he asked. "We can hit the casinos, plays some blackjack while we are there, and you can meet my mom."

I said sure. When we arrived at Doris's house in Vicksburg, she wanted to go with us to the casinos. The three of us played a few hands of blackjack and had a wonderful dinner. Then we went back to her house and stayed up until about three-thirty in the morning talking about her sons and the wonderful times they had shared when all the boys were wrestling. Fritz had his private pilot's license and owned his own plane, so the family would fly together from show to show. "We had so much fun as a family back in those days," Doris recalled.

Things had not been so rosy since the divorce. Doris had suffered two heart attacks but still smoked two packs of cigarettes a day. Her most recent heart attack happened less than a year before Kevin introduced us. Her doctor had warned her to quit smoking and take better care of herself; they warned her that the next heart attack would more than likely be her last.

The next morning, Kevin and I drove back to Dallas. I really enjoyed that night, which was the first of many trips Kevin and I would make to Vicksburg. Each trip seemed more interesting than the next. We would spend hours going through the family's "hope chest," where Kevin's mom had stored pictures, newspaper articles, and all the other mementos she had collected during all the years Fritz and their sons had been in the wrestling business, and each memento came with a story.

Later, after Kevin's mom arrived from Mississippi to see Fritz in the hospital, Kevin came to my house and told me how glad he was to see his mother and father together again, even if it was only for a short time.

One day while visiting Fritz at the hospital, I ran into Doris, who was on her way back to the hotel. She told me that driving to Dallas to see Fritz in the hospital was the hardest thing she had ever done. She had once said, while Kevin and I were visiting her in Vicksburg, that she felt guilty about leaving Fritz and wished things had been different. "I had to get away on my own and think about all that had taken place in my lifetime; a person just cannot deal with losing their children," she'd said. Doris told me that she would be staying at the Holiday Inn in Denton. "I am going to stay for as long as I can just in case there's something I can do to make Fritz's life a little better in his final days." She also told me the only reason she came to Dallas was that Kevin had called to say that Dad wanted to see her before he died.

Kevin told me earlier that many years ago he had gotten his brother David and his father through a rough patch with a similar trick. "Shortly after David first started professional wrestling," Kevin said, "he and Dad got into a really bad argument." Kevin said he could not remember all the details, but that it had something to do with the Sportatorium and the upcoming wrestling matches. "The argument was so bad that David told Dad that if he felt that way, then he was leaving Texas and would just go and wrestle somewhere else. The next day, David packed his bags and left for parts unknown.

"I was out of state at the time all this happened and did not learn about the argument until arriving back home two days after David left Denton. He had given Mom a letter to give to me. In the letter, David told me that he was leaving Texas for parts unknown and would get in touch with me later. I would not hear from him for over two months. Then one day, I get a letter from David saying he's fine and is wrestling in Florida. He wanted me to come and see him the first chance I got. The whole family really missed David." Kevin added, "Dad missed him, too, but I could never get him to admit it. Things had not been the same since he left.

"I had so many things going on in my life at the time that I could not leave right away, so I called some friends in Florida who were able to give me a phone number where I could get in touch with Dave. I tried my best to get him to come back to Dallas," Kevin said, "but he said he was not coming back until Dad apologized to him. I later tried to talk to Dad, but he and David were so much alike that neither one would give an inch.

"One day, I decided that I was tired of everyone asking me where my brother Dave was, so I came up with this plan to get David to come back to Dallas. I called WCCW's travel agent and got a first-class, one-way ticket to Dallas from Miami. I told our travel agent that David would pick the ticket up at the airport and to put on the ticket that it was purchased by Dad. I even gave him dad's credit card number so it would look as if Dad had purchased the ticket. I then called David and told him that Mom and Dad missed him and wanted him to come back to Dallas.

"'Dad told me to tell you that he is very sorry for what happened between the two of you, and if you come back to Texas he would be willing to forget everything and never mention it again,' I told him. Then, I jumped in the car and drove to the Sportatorium and had a talk with Dad. I told him that I had just gotten off the phone with David. 'Dad,' I said, 'David is in Florida and wants to come home. He said for me to tell you that he is sorry for what happen between the two of you and he is willing to forget everything and never mention it again.'

"It worked!" Kevin recalled. "A week later, David showed back up in Dallas, he and Dad never discussed the argument again, Dad gave David a big hug when he walked in the door, and all was forgotten. Two weeks after David came home, Gorgeous Jimmy Garvin and his valet, Sunshine, showed up at the Sportatorium looking for work. David had met them while wrestling in Florida and offered them a job wrestling for WCCW in Dallas, after he thought Dad had apologized. I guess Dad was glad to have David back home because he never said anything about the wrestlers who suddenly started showing up from Florida looking for jobs.

"Well, I guess my plan worked again," Kevin said. "When I left the hospital, Mom and Dad were getting along fine, laughing and talking as if they had never been apart."

Another week passed by before Kevin brought his father home from the hospital. I arrived at Fritz's house in time to hear Kevin and Doris offering to hire a live-in nurse to take care of Fritz during his cancer treatments. Doris had decided that she needed to go back to Mississippi and this had irritated Fritz; as I walked in the door he was cursing and yelling. "I am not going to spend my last few months on Earth being taken care of by someone I do not even know, and probably won't like anyway," he shouted. That is when I volunteered to move in with Fritz and do what I could to help. He agreed that if someone needed to look after him, he would rather it be someone he knew. "If you do not mind, Ron, that would be great," he said. So, about the middle of July, I locked up my house in Irving and moved in with Fritz.

A new routine began. Once a week, Kevin would take his father to Baylor Hospital for chemotherapy. With each treatment, Fritz seemed to get weaker and weaker. He looked terrible; his hair started falling out about two weeks into the treatments, so he had me shave his head.

After Fritz's chemotherapy treatment one day, a nurse approached Kevin with some advice. "Please, do not tell anyone I told you this," she said, "but if you can get your dad to smoke some marijuana, it might help him build up an appetite and make him feel a little better. Texas law does not allow the use of medical marijuana, nor can anyone here at Baylor recommend its use, even though chemotherapy patients seem to benefit from the property found in marijuana," the nurse said.

"I could get into trouble for telling you this so please keep it between you and me. It is just that I just hate to see someone suffer when there is something out there that can build up their appetite and ease their suffering just a little."

Fritz had burst out laughing when Kevin told him what the nurse had said on the way home from Baylor that morning. Fritz had been opposed to marijuana all his life. He had constantly yelled at his boys to stay away from it and had even spoken out at high schools and church meetings. Fritz had read that marijuana could ease the side effects of chemotherapy, but he was still skeptical. "Even if I agreed to smoke some, where would I get it?" he asked Kevin. "I think Ron could find you some," Kevin replied. "I will talk to him and see what we can do."

Later that day, Kevin came over to his dad's house and asked if I would like to go to Lake Dallas for a swim. That was when he explained to me what the nurse had said. "If you could get some pot, I am sure we could convince dad to try it," he said. I told Kevin I would have no problem getting my hands on some pot, but I would have a problem firing up a joint and handing it to his dad, who I knew had always spoken out against drug use. Nonetheless, I made a few phone calls and found a friend who had some very strong hydroponic marijuana. I went to get it, and as I drove back to Denton I could not get over the fact that I had just picked up some pot and was fixing to get Fritz Von Erich stoned. I had smoked pot several times in my life and had nothing at all against it. However, to pull some out and offer it to Fritz would take a little thinking about.

I took the pot over to Fritz's house and hid it in my room for a few days, hoping that Kevin would come by and mention it to his dad. That was not to be. When I asked Kevin one afternoon if he was going to come over and smoke some with us, he just looked at me. "Ron, I am sorry, but this is something that you will have to take care of. I could never sit in the same room with my dad and smoke pot. I hope you understand." I said, "Thanks a lot, Kevin."

I finally brought the subject up to Fritz late one night after he had not eaten anything the entire day. He and I had just finished drinking some Scotch when he told me his stomach was getting upset. I decided to tell him about the pot, saying I thought it would settle his stomach and make him feel better. He laughed and said he would try it, adding, "But I want you to know that all my sons would roll over in their graves if they knew what I was about to do."

I lit up a joint and handed it to Fritz, telling him to take a large hit and hold it in his lungs as long as he could before blowing it out. I just wanted him to have a couple of hits to get him feeling better, but before I knew it, I was stoned and we had smoked more than half a joint (and as I mentioned before, it was very strong pot).

"Do you feel any better now?" I asked Fritz.

"Yes," he said. He was silent for a moment. "Do you mean to tell me that is all there is to this stuff?" After I nodded my head, Fritz finally said, "I cannot believe I have had my head stuck in the sand all these years over this. What is the big deal, anyway? I thought I was going to see things and run around the house naked singing love songs." After another moment of laughter, he said, "Damn, Ron, I'm hungry."

I was thrilled, and asked him what he wanted to eat. "Something sweet," he said. After going through all the cabinets in his kitchen, Fritz finally decided on some pancakes with as much maple syrup and butter as I could put on them. We spent most of that night in the kitchen, laughing our heads off as I fixed Fritz one thing to eat after another. I had not heard him laugh so much since we met. He was sitting at the table while I was up cooking when he began laughing hysterically. "What is so funny?" I asked. Fritz stopped laughing for a moment and stared at me with a blank look on his face. "I forgot," he said, and then the laughter started over again. When he finally went to bed at about 3:00 a.m., he had a huge smile on his face; the next morning he told me he had slept better that night than he had in the last few years.

"Where did you get that pot we smoked last night?" he asked.

"From a friend in Dallas," I said.

"Do you think he can get some more?" Fritz said with a big grin on his face. I told him that it would not be a problem, and he seemed to perk up a little.

I cannot tell you how good it felt to see Fritz acting like his old self that morning. He was already up and around when I woke up and he clearly felt much better than he had the morning before, all because I had talked him into trying some marijuana. After that night, Fritz made a point of telling everyone who came by the house to see him that Ron had turned him into a "pothead." One of the neighbors even made him a roach clip to hold joints that he had smoked down to stubs.

During this time, Fritz really started opening up to me about all the hard times he had faced in his life. More than ever, he told me that he wanted me to write that book about him, so all his fans could get the true story about him and his family.

"Over the years, many writers have approached me with offers to tell my life story," Fritz said. "And, I guess I turned them all away. I did not want to talk about the death of my sons—do people not understand the hurt that all of us went through during those times? I have always felt that no matter what you tell a writer, most will add a few pages of BS just to make the story more interesting. I have read so many articles about my family that were nothing more than hearsay.

"I have heard of rumors and gossip in the past saying that I caused the deaths of my sons," he continued. "People say I pushed my boys too hard and too fast. I have read stories about me forcing the boys into wrestling so I could build my empire, and that is just not the case.

"Ron, I made sure that my boys were in good shape and healthy," Fritz told me. "I grew up believing that exercise is the best medicine for teenage boys growing up in the country with little else to do. It gives them something to look forward to when school is out and it keeps them out of trouble. Doris and I would encourage the boys to try out for any school sport of their choice. Doris was at every game or event cheering them on, and I would try to be there every chance I could.

"I loved my boys more than life itself. Ron, I would take those boys with me when I went overseas, as long as they were out of school. As a family, Doris and I would always set aside times for all of the family to be together. I would like all the Von Erich fans and the rest of the people around the world who read your book to know that Doris and I did the best we could raising our sons.

"I would like for the fans to be able to read for themselves about all the hard times as well as the good times, and to understand that I had nothing to do with those three boys taking their lives. I made mistakes just as every other parent in this world has, and if I had it to do all over again, I would do many things different. However, for what it's worth, Doris and I raised those boys as best we could."

I kept trying to tell Fritz that I did not know the first thing about writing a book. I tried to explain how I dropped out of school my sophomore year and went into the Marine Corp. English was always my worst subject; I do not think I ever passed high school English. That was not an excuse that Fritz would accept. He would keep telling me to take good notes and do the best I could.

"I know you will write a book I will be proud of," Fritz said. "Besides, Ron, there was a time when I thought I could not learn to use a computer, but you showed me that I was wrong. I know that if you will just try, you will succeed. Will you promise me that you will write my book?"

I made Fritz a promise that day and started taking those notes the best I could as Fritz recalled story after story about himself and his family's life together. Now, here I sit—doing my best to put together something Fritz would find worthy of his approval.

CHAPTER 2

Here is Fritz's story, told in his own words:

I was born on August 16, 1929 in Leon County, Texas, during the Great Depression. My father was a deputy sheriff and my mother a homemaker, and I the only child.

My best friend in the world was my granddaddy, Ross Adkisson. We had many great times together. When I was growing up in Jewett, the two of us were always going hunting, fishing, or maybe just going for a walk in the woods. Due to the amount of his influence, I fell in love with the outdoors and all it had to offer.

The earliest memory I have of my mother and father is of me riding around in my father's sheriff car. In those days, it seems my dad's main job was hunting down moonshiners. I was seven years old at the time. Dad and I would get home at all hours of night while my mother would be awake and walking the floors. I can picture her now, standing in the doorway, screaming at my father. She would tell him that I was just a little boy and he was going to get me killed one day.

When I was around eight years old, I remember playing a joke on my father. We lived in a small frame house in the country, and did not have running water. Our bathroom was an outhouse located 150 feet or more from our house in the woods.

Father had tied a string to the corner of our house that led to the outhouse for those late night and early morning visits. Every morning at 4:30 a.m. on the dot, father would wake up and follow that string to the outhouse. Late one evening, I thought how funny it would be to move that string about seventy-five feet away from the outhouse into the thickest part of the woods. After struggling to get up enough courage, I did it. Following supper that night, I went to bed laughing to myself and thinking about my father arriving in the woods early that next morning instead of the outhouse.

That next morning at around 4:40 a.m., father came back in the house and yanked me out of my bed. It was then that I received the worst spanking I had ever had in my life. It had started raining early that morning in January and was exceptionally cold. Seems old Dad had roamed around in the woods for a while before finding his way back to the house and my bed.

Our family moved from Jewett to Dallas when I was nine years old. I hated Dallas at first. The city was nothing like what I was used to. I really missed my Granddaddy Ross and all the good times we shared together in Jewett. I cannot remember why my family moved to Dallas. I do remember begging my mother and father to please let me stay with Granddaddy Ross, but that was not to be.

I was about twelve years old when Granddaddy Ross passed away. I loved that old man so much. He not only taught me to hunt and fish but he also taught me respect for the woods and all of God's creatures that live there.

My Granddaddy Ross and I would go duck hunting every chance we got. Duck hunting has always been a big part of my life and my family's life due to him. When all my sons were growing up, I would take them all duck hunting with me as often as I could. My whole family loved the outdoors and hunting. Doris would even go with us on occasion. I taught my sons to respect the outdoors, just as my father and Granddaddy Ross taught me. Every one of my sons grew up loving to hunt and fish just as I did when I was growing up.

In Dallas, I went to Crozier Tech High School. My track coach was my Uncle Rosy and he taught me to throw the discus and putt the shot. I learned to train hard and to take care of my body. Uncle Rosy was always telling me I was going to make a great athlete some day and could really go somewhere if I would just try hard. Try hard I did. I became an All-City defensive tackle and was All-State in track. I learned to love sports as much as I loved the outdoors. After high school, I accepted an athletic scholarship to Southern Methodist University in Dallas, turning down a music scholarship to the University of Texas.

At this point, Fritz interrupted his narrative to ask if I could guess what musical instrument he had played. After thinking about this for a moment and trying to picture Fritz Von Erich playing a musical instrument, I had to tell him I did not have a clue. He smiled at me and said, "The clarinet."

I really thought Fritz was pulling a joke on me. I sat back and waited for the punch line, but it never came. Fritz had indeed played the clarinet. What's more, he was a very good musician.My mother got me interested in music. She loved music, especially the horn instruments. One of my friends who lived close to us in Dallas played the clarinet and I picked it up from him.

My mother would encourage me to practice and took a real interest in my music, oftentimes getting upset with me if I tried skipping practice. She really wanted me to take that music scholarship at University of Texas, but I loved sports too much.

I started my first year at SMU playing football for the fresh man team. That year in track, I set the national freshman discus record and was a sure thing to win the Southwest Conference title for the next two years. I started for the varsity team my sophomore year. All the work I had put into track and football in high school and all the training that my Uncle Rosy had given me all those years was really starting to pay off. Not only was I winning one competition after another, but also, I was realizing I loved sports just as much as I loved the outdoors.

My junior year at SMU, I found a new love that was even stronger than both football and track. That is when I met a high school student named Doris Smith. She was seventeen and just graduating high school when we met for the first time. Doris had been considering enrolling at SMU and was best friends with one of the sophomore girls already enrolled there. Next thing I knew, I was head-over-heels in love with her. In fact, I was so much in love that I could barely think of anything else. Nothing meant much to me anymore—not football, track, hunting, or fishing. Just this girl named Doris Smith.

Doris was an East Dallas girl who was just graduating from Woodrow Wilson High School in Dallas. We had known one another for only a short time before both of us decided that we wanted to get married. I knew right away that Doris was the right girl for me, but I was playing football for Coach Mattie Bell, who had this rule barring players from getting married. If Doris and I tied the knot, I would lose my scholarship.

I loved going to school and playing ball for SMU, but I loved Doris even more. My grades started dropping and I had gotten to the point where all I cared about was Doris. I made up my mind that I wanted to marry her more than I wanted to stay at SMU and play ball. I thought I was a bit smarter than everyone and could do both. After many sleepless nights, I finally came up with a plan that I felt would work. If I could keep the marriage a secret for the next two years, until I graduated, I felt everything would be fine. While going over my new plan with Doris and talking with her parents, we started making plans that would give us both what we wanted.

One Friday night, Doris, her mother, brother, and sister and I all took off to Denton, where we were to be married by the Justice of the Peace in a small and very secret ceremony with only Doris's family as witnesses. Afterwards, Doris and I drove north out of Denton and rented a small cabin on the Texas side of Lake Tacoma for a brief honeymoon.

Late Sunday evening, after we arrived back in Dallas, I pulled into a gas station to fill up with gas while Doris went to the ladies room to freshen up. It was just a few minutes later when Doris came walking up to me with a strange sort of smile on her face. She handed me the *Dallas Morning News*; the headline read, "Adkisson Loses Scholarship at SMU." My heart skipped a beat as I stared at that newspaper. Seems some damned reporter had seen my name on a Denton County marriage certificate and had called SMU to verify that it was that Jack Adkisson. After SMU found out about us getting married, they decided to make an example of me by revoking my scholarship. Coach Bell was furious with me. He hated taking away my scholarship and told me so. Coach Bell said I was too good an athlete to let our marriage ruin my future, so he set me up with a tryout at the University of Kentucky, where Coach Bear Bryant was coaching at the time.

When I arrived at the University of Kentucky one week later, Bear did not even seem to notice me. However, after my first tryout later that day, he sure did. I was faster than most of his running backs and when I threw the discus I threw it farther than the Southeast Conference record. Once he saw what a good athlete I was, he came after me with a big smile on his face. Bear told me that he would give Doris a job in the athletic department and help us out any way he could. Doris and I hated to leave Texas where our families lived. I told Coach Bryant I needed a little more time to think about his offer and talk it over with my wife.

I drove back to Dallas early the next morning to think about my options. At one point, I decided to take a trip to Corpus Christi to visit an old friend who I had grown up with in Dallas and to check out the University there. The college campus at Corpus was the most beautiful school I had ever seen. It was surrounded by woods with wildlife everywhere I looked. After leaving the admission office, I decided to take a walk around the campus and check everything out. Once I walked through the woods for about fifteen minutes, I came out at a large bay behind the school. What I saw made my mouth water: ducks were everywhere I looked, and the fish were tearing up the top of the water, feeding. When I saw how great the hunting and fishing would be in the bay around the university, and all the wildlife around the city, I enrolled at the university on the spot. I have never seen so many ducks and geese! The bay was loaded with so much wildlife I could hardly believe my eyes. I was like a little kid in a candy store; after I saw all the wildlife there, I had to enroll. There was just too much good hunting and fishing to be done in this small town for me to pass up.

Therefore, I came back to Dallas and sort of lied to Doris. Alternatively, let us just say that I did not tell her about all the ducks and geese I had seen out there on the bay that morning. I just said I thought we would be happier in Corpus Christi. Therefore, early in 1952, we loaded up my old 1941 Black Mercury and headed south for whatever awaited us in Corpus Christi, Texas.

Both Doris and I enrolled at the University of Corpus Christi. Times were hard. We were so poor that we lived in an old army barrack on campus where we slept on a mattress on the floor. We were so much in love that we really did not care as long as we were together.

After attending the first semester at Corpus, I really started to hate going to that school. The college was very strict on everyone, even married couples. We were not allowed to kiss or dance on campus. Hell, they would not even let men and women swim in the same swimming pool together. I did not stay in the school's good graces for long. Only a few weeks went by before a school administrator busted me for kissing my wife goodbye before class. This had made me so angry that Doris and I both left the university shortly after that, but we stayed in the town of Corpus Christi for almost a year. The good friend whom I had first came to Corpus to visit owned a bait and tackle shop, so we stayed with him and his wife a while until we could come up with enough money to find something of our own.

I was working two jobs at the time, and I think Doris even worked two jobs at some point. Since we were living with my friend and his wife, we were able to save every penny we made. It was at this time that Doris started wanting a house of her own, and I had my mind set on getting her one. Making a trip back to Dallas one weekend, I made a deal with an old teammate of mine from SMU, Kyle Rote. We had known each other for quite a few years and he had this GI home loan coming. Kyle's father had helped Kyle and his wife buy a nice house, so Kyle was not going to use his GI loan. The two of us talked it over, then I gave him a couple of hundred dollars so he could get a low-cost VA loan to build a house in his name. When the house was completed, he sold us the two-bedroom, one-bath home for what it had cost him. Doris and I both fell in love with that little house.

We each got a dog after moving into our new home. I have always enjoyed having a good hunting dog. My dog at the time was a golden retriever named Rebel that I had spent many hours and weekends training. Doris had a mutt she named Pumpkin. She had found the little puppy abandoned on the side of the road and refused to part with it. I would be out in the backyard training Rebel and I would tell Rebel to retrieve Pumpkin. Rebel would run over, pick up Pumpkin by the back of her neck, and bring her to me. That damned puppy would start yapping and the next thing I knew Doris would be screaming at me and chasing me around the house. Seems her and the dog did not think that our little trick was that funny.

There was a loan company in Corpus Christi. As a second job, I worked as a collector for them. Since I was a big guy and everyone knew I had played football at the university, I made an offer to the old man who owned the collection company one day. If he would give me his toughest accounts, and if I could collect them, I would get to keep half the money. It took me a few weeks to finally convince the old man that I really needed the money and would give it my all. One day he finally gave in, saying that he would give me a chance and maybe I would get lucky.

For a while, I did pretty well. I would find these people real late at night or early in the morning right after they were paid. In those days, companies would always pay in cash. I would try to collect as much money as I could from them. Sometimes I played the role of a big tough guy who would gladly beat someone's ass if the boss did not get his money. Other times I would tell the guy that I was his last hope, that if he did not pay me, the owner would have the boys from New York come down and have a little talk with him. I would threaten, lie, or do just about anything legal back in those days to get money out of these people.

Things started to get dire after a few months when some of the people I was pressuring started to fight back. When money is tight, people do crazy things. I was shot at and threatened numerous times. Once, Doris and I came home to find cuss words painted on the side of our new house and all of our windows broken out. Right after that, Doris put her foot down and said she was not going to live like that. She began to get scared to stay in the house by herself so I gave up that job and went to work for the local fire department. I was working twenty-four hours on and twenty-four hours off, and I liked it because it gave me plenty of time for hunting and fishing. Then something happened that made me think about pursuing a different career.

I had not been working for the fire department long when I started hearing rumors that Texas was going to get a professional football franchise. Following weeks of phone calls, I finally ended up getting a tryout for the team. That meant I had to go to training camp and hope for an offer once I completed camp. Doris and I packed up the Mercury and boarded up the house. I quit the fire department, Doris quit her job, and we headed back to Dallas.

I went on to training camp in Kerrville, Texas, and Doris moved in with her mother. While I was in training camp one day, a phone call came in for me. Someone had taken a message and left it taped to my locker door. The message had been from Doris; she had been trying to get word to me that we would be having a baby soon. I was thrilled, and the news made me try even harder to be the best ball-player I could.

As it turned out, this new Dallas franchise was an ill-fated attempt to bring pro football to Dallas. Hard as it is to believe now, in 1952 the Dallas area was not yet ready for a pro-ball club. Regions were loyal to their respective colleges and television had not yet made its enormous impact on football. When the New York Yankees baseball team owner, Ted Collins decided to sell his NFL franchise back to the league after years of losing his ass, the league later sold the franchise to Texas millionaire Giles Miller, who relocated the team to Dallas, Texas.

Miller believed the football-crazy state of Texas was a perfect spot to locate an NFL franchise. After all, every major high school and college in the state was packing its stadiums to the hilt with crazed football fanatics. So the Dallas Texans were born—not to be confused with the Dallas Texans of the 1960s, who later became the Kansas City Chiefs. The Texans played in the 75,000-seat Cotton Bowl, but rarely attracted more than 15,000 fans. Unfortunately for Miller, the Dallas football fans were content with their college football teams and few of them turned out for Sunday NFL games. The lack of attendance caused cash flow problems for Miller, and with five games remaining in the season, the Texans were unable to meet payroll. The Dallas franchise was returned to the NFL and the league took over operations for the rest of the season.

The Texans did not fare much better on the field than they did off the field. They were considered the joke of the league and could manage just one win in twelve games. They became known as the worst NFL team ever.

I played in a few exhibition games until a bad knee sidetracked my career and the Texans went on without me. They would later move to Baltimore, where they became the Baltimore Colts. I loved football, but in those days the money just was not there, and I was afraid that if I did stay with the team I might not be paid. There had been so many rumors floating around in training camp that no one knew from one minute to the next how long the Texans would last. With a hurt knee, I was not sure how long the Texans would keep me on the roster. Therefore, I headed back to Dallas and started searching for another job.

One day, I received a phone call from Doc Sarpolis and old wrestling veteran named Ed Lewis, who then wrestled under the stage name of Strangler Lewis. They thought I had a good name in town since I had been a big athlete at SMU. Doc said that I might be able to draw a crowd as a professional wrestler and to come on down to the Sportatorium in Dallas for a meeting if I was interested.

Not once in my entire life had I ever considered becoming a professional wrestler. However, it sure beat dodging bullets for a living, or trying to collect a past-due bill, or putting my life on the line trying to put out a fire somewhere. I had a wife to support and a baby on the way; the income that Doc said I could make sounded good. With my knee now being a factor in my future, I had also started thinking that football was no longer for me. I have always felt that I could have made the team; my knee was not that bad. I loved playing football more than anything else I had ever done. Nevertheless, I had money on my mind and a plan to go on to improved things.

The first Saturday morning I showed up at the Sportatorium, I met three other guys that I would be training with. Strangler Lewis walked in the door later and told us all to have a seat; Strangler advised the three of us that for the next few days we would all be in the classroom getting to know one another and making sure that becoming a professional wrestler was what we really wanted to do with our lives.

Over the next few months, this man, who was now in his early sixty's, Ed "The Strangler" Lewis, would become my friend and mentor. Strangler, whose real name was Robert Herman Julius Friedrich, told the four of us about the wild and exciting world of "professional wrestling" and all the places he had traveled over his long and profitable career. As I think back on those early days now, Ed Lewis had a lot to do with me later coming up with my own hold, the "Iron Claw."

I will never forget some of the stories Ed relayed to us while we were training. "Early in my wrestling career," Ed told us, "I originated my very own hold that I named the 'Headlock.' I was convinced that the human brain would yield to pressure, and if lots of pressure was consistently applied, it would constitute a knockout just as if a boxer had landed a solid punch to the jaw. I had a wooden facsimile of a human head made for me to practice on. It was split down the middle with the two halves connected by very strong steel springs. To increase the power of my grip I practiced on this thing for hours at a time until I developed a grip that could crack a skull, but it was not a stranglehold. Never in my career was I ever disqualified for strangling an opponent.

The hold, however, was applied so close to the jaw that it looked like a stranglehold. The pressure was on the head, through the jaw. My hold took a bit longer than a boxer's blow to the jaw, but it had the same result. The tremendous pressure that I would apply to my opponent's head would stop the flow of blood to the brain until they passed out."

Ed would go on to tell us of the other great wrestlers that had made a name for themselves with their own holds, such as Frank Gotch, who came up with a toe-hold, which could break a man's leg, and did on several occasions. "In fact," Ed told us, "I have always thought that the hold Frank Gotch invented and perfected, started the move towards wrestling holds that, through intense pain and the threat of a broken arm or leg, would cause your opponent to give up when there was no chance of winning."

Joe Strecher, another great wrestler, came up with the body-scissors, a leg-hold that could crush the bones his legs were wrapped around. Joe invented this leg grip himself, and added strength to his legs by wrapping them around 50-pound bags of grain on his Kansas farm and squeezing until the bags burst. This was a killer hold, and once Joe Strecher applied it on his opponent, there would be very little doubt about the outcome of the match.

Ed Lewis was one hell of a wrestler. He won the World Belt four times in his career and was later named the first commissioner for the sport of wrestling. Ed had to leave Dallas and go back up north about seven months into my career due to medical problems. He had been having problems with his eyes the entire time he spent in Dallas and would later go totally blind.

I guess Ed Lewis had more to do with my success than anyone I can think of. All the things Ed told us about how to become a wrestling star stuck with me throughout my career.

I trained for several months during the late afternoons and worked as a security guard at night before my first live wrestling match. Two days before the match, I broke my shoulder in a practice match at the Sportatorium. I was thrown from the ring over the top rope and landed on the hard cement floor. In those days, there were no mats on the floor to break your fall as in today's matches. Missing that first match did not bother me as much as missing that paycheck, especially with our baby on the way. I was desperate for money, so I went to work as a bookkeeper for the local wrestling promoter. The job did not pay all that much, but I planned to be in the ring as soon as my shoulder healed. It seemed that this wrestling idea was starting to get in my head.

When I finally got my chance in the ring, I lost thirteen matches in a row. I think I set an all-time record for the most losses for someone trying to start a new career. The large payoffs I had heard so much about did not happen at that time.

Even so, wrestling had started to get into my blood, so I tried harder. To hear fans cheer for me instead of for a whole team was wonderful. I vowed to myself that I would not give up on what would probably be my last chance for a career in sports.

I decided that my best bet would be to let Doris stay with her mother while I headed up north to Boston and other parts of New England to get wrestling experience. However, even though I was working hard, Doris and I were as poor as a married couple could be. I felt like I was going to starve to death at times. I think I was eating Boston-baked beans for breakfast, lunch, and dinner because I could buy them for twenty-nine cents a plate. We still had that baby on the way and I was trying to send Doris all the money I could, but there just was not much to send. My friend in Corpus was trying to sell our two-bedroom, one-bath home that we had decided to leave behind.

Doris later moved into a duplex on Hall Street in Dallas next to my grandmother and was paying forty-five dollars a month in rent. That was a bit high in those days but Doris was close to my grandmother, so I felt better that she was not by herself. It was while I was in Boston that I wrestled for that three dollars a match, and I was very glad to get it in those days.

It was a challenge for me to stay on track and keep my mind focused on the goal of becoming a professional wrestler. On the other hand, after being a wrestler for a while, I developed an attitude that helped me prevail through thick and thin. I realized after a time in the business that there was no fan on Earth more dedicated than a wrestling fan. That became my inspiration and made me try harder; I really loved the wrestling fans.

It seemed like I was in Boston forever, but it was only three short months. I missed Doris so much and I knew our baby would be coming along anytime. I finally made it back to Dallas, but sadly I had to leave shortly afterward to go to Des Moines. This time, though, I packed up Doris and took her on the road with me.

We knew it would be hard for both of us with the baby due soon, but I had made up my mind that I needed her love and support to help me through the hard times. I was also looking forward to our new baby, and was hoping for a boy so I would have someone to take hunting and fishing with me.

When I was wrestling in Boston, I would oftentimes feel guilty about being away from my family all the time. At night, I would dream about Doris and the large family we would have some day, and the new house we would own—a large house, with a few good hunting dogs, and plenty of land and woods for all my children to roam around on.

Dreaming about Doris and our life together made it hard for me to keep my mind on becoming a professional wrestler. I cannot tell you of the countless times I almost gave up on my dream and caught a train back home. In this business, if your mind is not in the ring with you, you can sure get hurt in a hurry. I felt this would be my last chance to make a career in sports, which was something I wanted more than anything in the world for myself and my family, so I tried hard not to let all the disappointments and setbacks stand in my way.

CHAPTER 3

After thirteen humiliating losses in a row on live television, my supporters in Dallas were starting to think I could not beat anyone. My friends and family were trying to get me to give up on wrestling, but I was determined to stick it out no matter what. Hell, both our families tried to get Doris to convince me to quit wrestling and try to get my job back with the fire department in Corpus Christi, since we were having problems selling our small house and would have a rent-free place to live. Nonetheless, Doris always stood up for me even when it seemed like I would never win. She by no means expressed a moment of doubt and her love and support is what kept me going night after night.

Though I was not winning any matches at all, the old-timers really started to resent the younger wrestlers who thought they could make a mark in the business. The majority of them were not shy about showing me who was boss in the ring. In order to protect myself from serious injury, I had to become a defensive-style wrestler in a hurry. I knew that before I could start winning matches I had to take my bumps like everyone else. It was just surviving those first few years that I was worried about. I could not afford to miss any more paychecks.

When I finally started winning a few matches, I decided to adopt a stage name. I made the decision one day while I was driving cross-country to yet another match. All the old-timers and new successful wrestlers in the business had colorful nicknames like Hard Boiled Haggerty, Stranger Lewis, The Atomic Blondes (who were Chet Wallich and Johnny "The Hammer" Valentine), Crusher Lisowski and Dick the Bruiser, Haystack Calhoun, and Gorgeous George just to name a few. These guys were all wrestling in main events, which meant they were making a lot more money than I was. A large amount of my matches were taking place up north, where no one had ever heard of Jack Adkisson the SMU football and track star. This was my chance to create a new name and to come up with some sort of personality that would make me a hit with all the wrestling fans.

Well, as everyone now knows I chose the name Fritz Von Erich. Fritz had been the name of a close family friend in my hometown of Jewett. I have always liked the manly sound of the name Fritz. Von Erich was my grandmother's maiden name. Her family was of German decent and I was a blonde-haired young man who looked German. Due to Adolph Hitler and World War II, most Americans still hated the Germans. Still, that did not bother me. The best way to make it in professional wrestling in those days was to get the fans to hate you. Every one of the promoters was big on the bad guys because they were the ones that attracted the crowds. Fans loved seeing the bad guys get creamed. At the time though, I did not realize that changing my name would alter my life and career forever.

After I changed my name to Fritz Von Erich, the local promoter decided I needed a costume to go along with my new identity. He loaned me enough money to have my first cape and ring jacket custom made just for me. Both my first ring jacket and cape were bright red with a large black German swastika on them. The custom-made cape and ring jacket set me back twelve dollars each. Then I added a pair of used, shiny, knee-high black German marching boots that cost another sixteen dollars and that I found in an Army & Navy store. My new wrestling attire cost a total of forty dollars, which I agreed to pay back to the promoter at twenty-five cents per match until the jacket, cape, and boots were paid for. To bring my new persona to life, I worked on my German goose step for hours every day and watched old War World II movies on television every chance I could. I would try my best to copy the mannerisms of the Nazi-era Germans. Numerous practice hours went by and I finally had my new role down and was ready to try it out on the fans. My main problem had been trying to sound German. No matter how hard I practiced I could not get rid of my deep Southern accent. Most of the time when a fan would ask me a question, I would just look at them and grunt, then walk away. This usually would prevent them from following me around and asking more questions.

During this time my first son, Jack Jr., was born and the word "family" took on a completely new meaning for me. I was the happiest new father in the world and already daydreaming about the day little Jack Jr. would be old enough to spend his days hunting and fishing with me. I was on cloud nine and more determined than ever to make something of my new career. That would turn out to be a whole lot easier said than done. Doris and I had to do without food sometimes while I was healing from what seemed like one injury after another. However, no matter how hungry Doris and I were, we always made sure little Jack Jr. had enough to eat. Many times I would be stuck in bed with some sort of injury and Doris would have to find a job and bring home the money until I healed.

When Jack Jr. was just a few months old, we moved back to Texas and settled in Fort Worth. Things had been going very well for me up north. However, Doris and I both were very homesick. We were getting letters from all our folks asking when they would be able to see Jack Jr. We found our way back to Texas and I found a job as a detective during the day and was wrestling at night. Unfortunately, there were mornings when I was in such pain I just could not get out of bed and go to work. One day, I dragged myself to work looking like a large truck had run over me. Actually, I looked like the truck driver who had run me over saw who it was, then backed the truck up, and ran over me a second time. That was the day my boss told me I had to choose between working for him and being a professional wrestler.

As a result, I quit my detective job that day and focused all my energy on reaching my dream of becoming a pro wrestler. I felt like the answer to all of our financial problems was for me to leave Texas again and head back up north. Wrestling paid better up north. Matches were bigger and there were much larger names there. Doris and Jack Jr. moved in with my mother-in-law on Mt. Auburn Street in East Dallas. Once I got Doris and the baby settled, I headed back to Boston, where I wrestled for a few months until I could scrape together enough money for an old motel apartment (which was just a motel room with a kitchen and its own bathroom) in Des Moines. I had started winning a few matches for a change, so I was finally ready for Doris and Little Jackie to join me.

I could not wait to meet the train in Des Moines that late September morning and see my baby and tell Doris that I felt I was finally on my way to achieving my dream. When that train stopped and Doris and Jack Jr. stepped off, I came walking up to them dressed in my first new gray flannel suit and a shiny new pair of blue suede shoes. When Doris saw me in that new suit, her mouth dropped open and I thought she was going to drop Jack Jr. on his head. I felt like a million dollars that day. I had even saved a little extra money so I could take Doris and little Jackie out on the town.

As things turned out, Doris and I were glad to be back together as a family again. On the down side, she hated the apartment I had picked out in Des Moines, even though it was the best I could do at the time.

Next door to our apartment was a man Doris described to me as a "dirty old man." He was a Peeping Tom who the manager's wife had warned her about after we moved in. The man would stand around in back of the apartment and keep scaring Doris, so she had a latch put on the door where you could only open it from the inside. When I was out of town wrestling, which seemed to be most of the time, she would keep the door latched. That was well and good, but when I got home late at night it was damn near impossible to wake her up. That woman could sleep though anything, including my loudest knocks and shouts. Finally, we came up with a system where she would put a paper clip in her hair, tie a string to the end of it and run the string out the door. When I came home late at night, I would just pull on the string, which would pull her hair and wake her up.

Well, this worked out fine until one night when I was riding home with a few other wrestlers. We had all stopped off at the local pub and had a few beers after the show. When they stopped at my place to drop me off, I decided I would be a smart-ass and said, "Hey guys, watch this." I walked up to the door and yanked very hard on the string. Well, Doris opened the door all right, calling me names I did not think my sweet little wife knew. The guys were all laughing their heads off of course. When Doris heard the laughter, she knew I was showing off for them and got even madder. I do not remember for sure, but I think I slept in a chair that night. We were much to poor to be able to afford a couch.

In Des Moines, my career started picking up somewhat. I was making good money as long as I was wrestling and not home recovering from one injury or another. I had some big matches scheduled in Minnesota so Doris, Jack Jr., and I all packed our bags and found another cheap motel in Minneapolis. We were all together and happy. Wrestling was becoming big all over the country, I was starting to get many matches and experience under my belt, and the money was getting much better as my experience grew.

I did well in Minneapolis until one night when Killer Stan Kowalski jumped off the top rope and landed on me with a knee to the back. I thought he had broken my back at first. After the match that night I managed to find my car and drive back to the motel. I tried to get out of the car but fell to the ground and could not get up. I finally was able to crawl up to the door that night and started scratching on the screen trying to get Doris to wake up so she could help me. The next morning, my back hurt so bad I could barely raise my arms; it took me about eight weeks to heal from that one. My back was not broken but had been bruised bad enough to keep me home in bed and out of the ring for a while. The money stopped coming in while I was recuperating and the hard times started all over again. Doris, bless her heart, had to start looking for another job.

I had healed and started wrestling again after a couple of months. Then things started picking up when I got an offer to go to Calgary in western Canada on a promise from a promoter of more money and better matches. The road trips were very long on that Trans-Canadian highway, but we drove through some of the most beautiful country I had ever seen in my life. There were lakes and rivers everywhere in Canada, so I always made sure I had my fishing rod on those trips, just in case the urge hit.

I had another good friend who owned Spartan Mobile Homes in Houston. We had been very close friends growing up as kids in Dallas and always stayed in touch with one another. I called him one day and asked him if he would sell us a mobile home and have it sent up to us in Canada. He said sure, and that since he and his family were in need of a vacation anyway and we had not seen each other in a while, he would just bring it up to me himself. Therefore, we agreed that I would pay all expenses for him and his family. Three weeks later, they made the trip and Doris and I had our first mobile home. It was thirty-seven feet by eight feet and it made moving from town to town much easier. In addition, when I got tired of driving I could just pull over at the nearest river or lake and take a nap. Doris just loved it (anything had to be better than motel rooms) and this gave little Jack Jr. a place he could call home.

We took the mobile home to the local promoter's land up in the Rocky Mountain foothills and parked it there. It was so beautiful in the mountains. Doris and Jack Jr. would stay at the trailer and I would leave in the car on Monday mornings. I would wrestle all over western Canada during the week and be back at the trailer on Friday evenings. On the weekends, Doris could use the car to go to town and buy groceries for the family.

At that time, wrestling was very big in Canada and getting even bigger. For the first time in my career, I began to taste stardom as I wrestled in such towns as Edmonton, Regina, Saskatoon, and Calgary. Oh! I better not leave out Moose Jaw.

The first time I wrestled in Moose Jaw was around the mid-1950s. The town was very small but it was the only place around for all the lumberjacks to go and let off steam on a weekend. Lumber was a very big business in Canada back in those days and the crowds that attended the matches were always large.

Most of the time, wrestling matches would take place indoors. However, on the day I arrived in Moose Jaw the only building that would hold a large enough crowds had been damaged in a recent storm. The promoters decided that the show must go on, so they set up a wrestling ring outside behind the high school in the middle of the baseball field. Metal chairs had been set up all around the ring for the fans, and we were ready to go. The matches were due to start at 7:00 p.m. sharp this particular night. However, at 6:45 p.m. the unthinkable happened; it started to rain, and I mean rain hard. The other wrestler and I kept looking out from the windows of the small trailer that had been set up as a dressing room behind the ring to see if anyone was sitting down, but every single seat was empty.

We were all thinking that they would cancel the matches that night due to the pouring rain and strong winds. However, it was not long before the promoter came walking in the door of the trailer and told us that all the chairs had been moved from around the ring. "The fans have started pulling their cars and trucks up to the ring instead of sitting in chairs in the rain," the promoter said. Then, in the background, we heard the announcer proclaim to all the fans that we would wrestle in fifteen minutes. We looked at the promoter who was still standing in the trailer as if he were out of his mind. It was forty degrees outside and turning into one hell of a storm. When we started to complain, the promoter simply looked at us and told us that if we did not feel we could wrestle that night, we could go and make the announcement to all the drunken lumberjacks out there, because he did not want to hear it. At 7:30 p.m., the fans who had pulled their cars and trucks up to the ring turned on their headlights started honking their horns, and we started the matches.

It was around this time in Canada that I came up with my own wrestling hold. This one hold would change my entire career. It was a wrestling hold that I would later name "The Iron Claw."

The idea for the Iron Claw came to me quite by accident. One night in a wrestling match in Edmonton I found myself in a rather compromising situation. All wrestlers know it as the mount position. It meant I was on my back with my opponent on top of me. He had wrapped his legs around my legs. His head was lying on my chest, tucked just under my chin. This guy had wrapped himself around me so tight I could not move. Not only could I not move, but also I could not get this guy off me no matter what I tried.

I had developed a very strong hand and forearm in college from throwing the discus for so many years. I had also built up the muscles in my fingers from griping the discus so hard before finally letting it fly. I was able to work my right arm free from his grasp, then reached over and put my hand around the top of his head. I only did this hoping it would push his head back far enough that the pain would cause him to remove his legs from around my legs. As I started pushing his head back as hard as I could, I naturally tightened my grip on his forehead, which caused me to dig my fingernails into the sides of his face. I was very surprised by this guy's reaction.

He started to scream in pain. Blood began to trickle down the side of his face and drops fell on my chest. The blood started at the soft, fleshy part above his eyebrow. The crowd came out of their seats screaming after seeing the blood. This caused me to tighten my grip even more. My opponent seemed to be in a daze, which allowed me to get him off me. Although I was not able to keep this new hold going that long, it was long enough for me to get him off me and get back on my feet.

Early that next morning, on my first plane trip to yet another city, I started thinking about that match. Thoughts just kept racing through my mind as I begin thinking about the way the crowd had reacted after seeing the blood running down my opponent's face, about the look of pain on this guy's face, and the loud cheers of the fans. I knew at that very moment I was onto something.

There was already a similar hold in wrestling that was known as the "Abdominal Claw." It had been around for a few years and was applied to the stomach area and was somewhat different from my claw. I began to go to work on my new idea, coming up with several exercises that I hoped would build the strength even more in my fingers and forearms. I would let my fingernails grow out longer than they already were, and keep them sharp on the ends. With the addition of this new wrestling hold, my transformation would be complete. I had now become Fritz Von Erich, "The Master of the Iron Claw." In those days, there were no gyms specifically for wrestlers to use for training. I was always moving from one town to another anyway, so I doubt I would have had much time to go to a gym. Instead, I devised my own exercises. Every chance I had I would squeeze a rubber ball to build up the muscles in my fingers. When I was home or in a hotel I would lay my hand flat on a desk or coffee table with my palm down. I would start stacking books up one on top of the other with my fingertips just under the edge of the books. Then I would raise my fingers up and down for as long as I could. This would work the muscle groups in my fingers and forearms. I kept adding books to the pile and soon I had a stack so high the books would keep falling over.

I was in a motel room in some town I cannot remember in Canada when I first came up with the name "Iron Claw." After a match one night, I got back to the motel and lay down across the bed. I was almost asleep with an old World War II movie on the old black-and-white television. I never knew the name of that movie but I remember that I kept hearing them talk about the Iron Cross. When I opened my eyes, I thought, *That's it; I will call my new hold the "Iron Claw."*

From that point on, I would come out of the dressing room wearing my red cape and black German marching boots. I started goose stepping out of my dressing room as the crowd's boos and sneers echoed in the building.

Once in the ring, I would grab my right wrist with my left hand and hold the "Claw" up for everyone to see. The announcers would introduce me to crowds as being from Berlin, Germany, telling everyone in the building that I had come to the United States to destroy all Americans.

The fans hated me and sometimes I would have problems getting out of the building to my car. I have had wrestling fans attack me on my way back to the dressing room after a big match. Once I had a fan jump from the top of the bleachers as I was passing under them on my way back to the dressing room, just barely missing me and landing on the hard cement floor. Another time, as I was making my way back to the dressing room, I felt a sharp pain in my butt. I kept looking down, trying to figure out what was hurting so bad, but the rowdy fans around me made me focus on just getting back to the dressing room. As I walked through the dressing room door I ask one of the wrestlers to take a look at my butt and see what was causing me so much pain. I heard him say, "Damn, Fritz. Hold on, buddy; this might hurt a bit," as he pulled a six-inch hat pin that was imbedded all the way up to the little round red ball on the end from my ass. I have had fans jump in the ring during a match and attack me, and have had fans throw everything from cups of ice to ringside chairs at me. At several cities, I even had to have the police escort me out of the building to a car that was waiting to get me away from the stadium. However, I knew this role was going to be my ticket to lots of money and the stardom that I craved.

The Iron Claw soon became one of the most feared holds in professional wrestling, and my career was starting to soar. My forearms and fingers became so strong from my special exercises that I had designed that when I applied the Iron Claw to my opponents' heads and squeezed with all I had, digging my fingernails into the upper parts of their faces, it would cut the blood flow to the brain off and bust them open every time. Sometimes the guy would just bleed profusely and the fans would come out of their seats. Since all wrestling fans love blood, the Iron Claw attracted big crowds at the box office. Wrestling fans from all over were lining up, eager to see if the big bad German with the Nazi death grip could be defeated.

I was bending silver dollars, popping off bottle caps, and ripping large phone books in half for the audience's benefit before the match began. There was no phony stuff involved because I had exercised the muscles in my hand and forearm to the point that I really was that strong. When most of the other wrestlers were pumping iron and running five miles a day, I was sitting in my motel room doing the hand and finger exercises that I had designed for myself. There were some days when I would do four hundred push-ups on my fingertips. On planes, trains, and buses when I was not able to exercise, I was squeezing that rubber ball that I kept with me at all times.

Following the naming of the Iron Claw, I went down to the patent office in Minnesota and had the name and the hold patented. I knew I was on my way to the top and I wanted to make sure that everyone knew the Iron Claw belonged to me.

In Canada, at that time, major wrestling was taking place in Toronto. If fans and promoters wanted you in Toronto that meant you had arrived in the business. Finally, the day came when I got the call. Believe me when I tell you I was done past ready for that phone call when it finally came.

At the Maple Leaf Gardens in Toronto, matches were televised live each week by network TV to every major market in Canada. Television was still in its infancy in the late 1950s and the country was looking for national stars. Naturally I wanted to be one of them, so Doris, Jack Jr., and I packed up our mobile home and headed for the big time in Toronto.

We finally decided to settle in at Niagara Falls after moving from one city to another—a beautiful city that we would call home for the next several years. That move became a giant step forward in my career. I became an instant success on Canadian national television. I was in very big demand all over Canada and the northern United States and the big money had finally started coming my way.

I got hold of my tag team partner from Calgary, Walter Von Sieber, and we began performing together in Toronto. He and I continued as tag team partners but this time on prime time national television as opposed to in Moose Jaw on a weekend. Most wrestling fans would later know Walter as Waldo Von Erich, my brother. Of course, he was not really my brother, but he had a German routine that I thought was a lot like mine and he and I had both started up north together, so we became the Von Erich brothers from Berlin.

When I pulled up at the Maple Leaf Gardens, the Toronto promoter was standing in the parking lot. He said he needed me to come up to his office for a minute. For a brief moment, I thought the worst of what could be. When we got up to his office, he told me to have a seat and then he started telling me how all the wrestling fans around the Toronto area really wanted to get a look at me and my feared Iron Claw. The promoter told me that they had really been building the publicity up on me for the past couple of weeks and were expecting record crowds at the box office.

Then he told me that it looked like I was going to be a big star there, and if I was going to be a star I had to look like one. He told me to go out and buy a Cadillac and some new suits. Well, I almost fainted. "A Cadillac!

I cannot afford a Cadillac," I said. That's when the promoter looked me in the eye, then told me I could not afford not to have a Cadillac. He gave me the name of a local Cadillac dealer in Toronto who just happened to be a friend of his, and I went down and financed a brand new Cadillac. When I got back to our trailer and told Doris, she could not believe it. That was when I told her that the payments were a $120 per month. I thought I would have to take her to the hospital; that was more money than I had made in some months.

Wrestling matches were very different back in those days. People in the audience did not wear jeans and t-shirts. In Toronto and New York, all the men sitting around ringside would be wearing suits and ties and the women would be dressed in their best dresses.

We settled in Niagara Falls, but were still very homesick for Texas. It had been a few years since Doris and I had seen our families, and since I was making good money, we loaded up the Caddy and drove down to Texas.

When we got back up north I tried Minnesota and St. Louis but soon returned to Niagara Falls, doing most of my wrestling in Canada. By this time, we had another addition to the family, a baby boy born in Belleville, Illinois whom we named Kevin Ross.

We were doing very well up north and things could not have been much better. One day I got a call from a promoter from Houston, Morris Siegel, who offered me a very good deal to come to Texas and wrestle. Doris and I were so homesick for all of our friends and family that we jumped at the chance. It seemed too good to be true. We had just traded in our old mobile home for a new fifty-foot by ten-foot mobile home, which I had to hire a truck and driver to pull down to Texas at a cost of more than one thousand dollars.

So, there we were with a very large car payment, mobile home payment, and a new baby, and we were heading down to Texas with neither of us knowing exactly what to expect. When we got to Houston, the deal fell apart. Morris Siegel had suffered a heart attack two days after we had talked on the phone. He had been admitted to the hospital after suffering from severe chest pains. The hospital had listed him in critical but stable condition, which meant that no one but family and the doctor could get in to see him. As it turned out, no one else had any prior knowledge of the deal Morris Siegel and I had made over the phone, which put Doris and I in a very bad situation.

At this point, we were desperate and scared. We had just spent almost all of our money getting everything down to Texas. We decided to head back to Dallas where we still had friends and family who could help us if we needed it. After arriving in Dallas, we parked our mobile home in the cheapest trailer park we could find. Doris and I decided that she and the two boys would stay in Dallas while I took off for Minnesota to start all over again.

In June 1958, after being on the road for what seemed like years, Doris called me to say her younger brother David was going into the hospital for a brain tumor operation. Seems that David had been sick the better part of his life. Doris was so upset that I dropped everything and rushed back to Dallas. I got there just in time for the operation. David never did come out of that hospital. His temperature began to climb and it never leveled off. The next day he passed away at the age of fourteen.

I later went back to Minneapolis, where my wrestling career was still doing well. I was working many main events and was starting to save enough money to get my family back together. I missed my wife and boys very much.

One month after Doris's brother died, she gave birth to another boy in Dallas. She named him David Allen after her little brother. She called to tell me the wonderful news as she was going back to her hospital room. I left Minneapolis and rushed right back to Texas. I could only stay a few days, so Doris, against my wishes, checked out of the hospital to be with me as long as she could. She had just given birth some twelve hours before I had arrived.

I was able to stay in Dallas for almost a week and then had to be in North Carolina to wrestle for at least four months. When I got back to Dallas, Doris presented me with a tax refund check of fifteen hundred dollars. We used that money to have our trailer moved back to Niagara Falls, where I knew there would be plenty of work for me.

By then I was really getting tired of spending so much time away from my family. When Doris and the boys got to Niagara Falls, Doris and I had a long talk. I told her I wanted to save as much money as we could and move back to Corpus Christi and open that bait and tackle shop on the Inter-Coastal Canal just outside of Corpus that we had talked about so many times. I was thinking that maybe I could wrestle part-time and fly in and out of Corpus for a while until the bait and tackle business could support itself. I still loved wrestling, but being away from my family all the time was really hurting me. Being with my wife and three boys was all I would think about. When you are in that ring thinking about something besides your opponent, it is a good way to get yourself hurt.

One night I drove home about two hundred miles from a wrestling match in Cleveland. When I got to our trailer in Niagara Falls, all the lights were on in our trailer and a crowd of people was gathered at the front door. I did not know at that time that the Pennsylvania and New York highway patrol had been searching for me all night.

My friend Gene Kiniski, the world heavyweight champion at the time, saw me pull up and walked out to the car. After opening the door and sitting down beside me, he put his hand on my shoulder and with tears in his eyes told me that my son, little Jack Jr., was dead. My first boy was seven years old when he died.

A man at the mobile home park had been trying to rewire his trailer and had accidentally left a bare wire hot. It had shorted out against the metal on the outside of the trailer. Little Jack Jr., on his way home from a friend's house, touched the side of the wet trailer and was electrocuted. The electrical currents knocked him out and he fell facedown in a puddle of water from the melting snow and had drowned. I was devastated. I had never felt the way I felt on that night. I could not accept the fact that my firstborn son, little Jack Jr., was dead. The pain that rushed through my body was unbelievable.

I looked at Gene, who was still sitting beside me in the car, and thought there must be a mistake. There was no mistake. A bright light flashed in my head and before I could stop myself I put my hand through the driver's side window, breaking the glass.

A moment passed and I remembered my wife and my other two boys, so I got out of the car. With blood dripping from my hand from the broken glass and tears streaming down my face, I went to find my wife, who just a couple of months before had lost her little brother. I found Doris in the trailer house, rolled up in a ball in the corner of our bedroom. Some neighbors were watching Kevin and David, and Doris had just returned from the hospital. We held each other in our arms that night and cried over the loss of our first son. That hurt worse than anything that had ever happened to me in my life. That night would change not only my personal life but my wrestling career as well.

Doris blamed herself for not looking out the window or going to check on little Jack Jr. I blamed myself for not being there to protect my family, for not being there to teach my sons about all the dangers they would encounter in this world while growing up. It stayed on my mind for years and years afterward. Even sitting here telling you my story today still stirs an emotion and hurt inside of me that have never gone away.

CHAPTER 4

After Jack Jr. died, I went back to wrestling up north, mainly because we needed the money. At the time of my son's death we did not have insurance and the funeral and other expenses left us pretty much broke. Doris and I decided we would do our best to save up enough money to move back to Texas, where we would buy that bait and tackle shop in Corpus Christi. We both wanted to give our remaining two sons a nice home. Moreover, we both thought that was the right future for us at the time.

I could not help but think that if I had cared more about my family and less about becoming a professional wrestler, maybe little Jack Jr. would still be alive. Kevin and David became more precious to me than ever, and it began to bother me when I had to pack my bags and leave my family for another week on the road.

My wrestling career really started to change after my first son passed away. It was a few weeks of doing nothing but thinking about the death of Jack Jr. and arriving back in New York State before I could climb back into the ring and start working again. I still felt so guilty about my oldest son's death that there were times I just wanted to die. Early in the mornings, after a match, when I was along driving to another city, I would start crying and have to pull the car over to the side of the road. Night after night I began to pour out my anger and frustration in the ring and my opponents took a beating because of it. The anger that had been building up in me every night since Jack Jr.'s death had made me unstoppable. After weeks passed, I guess in the back of my mind I just started blaming the entire wrestling business for the death of my oldest boy, and for the first time in my career I started to look forward to climbing back into that squared circle and going after one of the guys who I held personally responsible for all my bad luck.

I got such a bad reputation for being overly aggressive in the ring that some wrestlers even turned down matches with me. The ones that did sign their name on that dotted line usually left the ring bloodied and battered. My new attitude may have been tough on myself and my opponents, but it was good for my career and the promoters. I was winning almost every match unless I was disqualified for one reason or another. I started doing better than I ever had managed to in the past, and to keep my mind off my family, I would work out until the early morning hours, getting my body in the best shape of my life. But no matter how hard I worked, I still felt empty and hurt inside, as if something had been ripped from my body.

A few short weeks after Jack Jr.'s death, Doris announced that we were going to have another baby. She wanted a daughter more than anything in the world and I really wanted her to have one. She had even picked out the name for our new little girl—Jill. To be honest, I wanted a little girl, too, but it was not to be. On February 3, 1960, Doris gave birth to a boy we named Kerry Gene Adkisson.

When Doris gave birth to Kerry, I do not think she was physically or emotionally over the loss of Jack Jr. or her brother David, for that matter. Kerry was born premature and we almost lost him at birth. He had to stay in an oxygen tent until he was strong enough to nurse. Kerry turned out to be a tough little kid and he battled back after about a month and started to gain weight.

By this time, I had been in the wrestling business for over nine years and was finally within spitting distance of something that resembled the top of my field. In mid-1961, I was in line for a shot at the American Wrestling Association's (AWA) World Heavyweight Championship title, which was held by Vern Gagna.

I was rated No. 3 in the world and was scheduled to wrestle the No. 2 man, Whispering Bill Watson—a very experienced and tough ex-world champion. This match would take place at the Buffalo War Memorial Auditorium in Buffalo, New York, and the winner of that match would go on to face Vern Gagna for the world title. It would be a very big match in front of a sold-out crowd and televised on national TV. The special guest referee would be the legendary Rocky Marciano, "The Brockton Bomber" himself. Marciano had been the only man ever to retire as the undefeated world heavyweight boxing champion and the fans up north loved him. Rocky had been retired from boxing only a few short years but was almost broke because of a very bad manager who had misappropriated much of his money. To make some extra cash, Marciano needed to do special guest appearances.

That night, in my dressing room, as I was getting ready for the match, my very good and close friend Gene Kiniski came back to wish me luck. He told me that he had overheard the New York fight promoter offering Marciano an extra thousand dollars if he would get in an argument with me during the match and knock me out in front of the crowd. This statement that had been made by this New York fight promoter angered me to no end. I knew

I would be in for a hell of a fight that night, but I was not that worried because in my mind I did not think either Marciano or Bill Watson could knock me out.

As the match was about to begin, I strode from the dressing room wearing my red cape and black German marching boots as I goose stepped down the aisle. As usual, the crowd booed and sneered and threw cups of ice and soda at me as I made my way to the ring surrounded by three Buffalo police officers. I grabbed my right wrist with my left hand after stepping onto the ring apron and begin to show my feared Iron Claw to the crowd. With a sneer on my face, I slowly began to turn in a circle so everyone could see. I stopped short when Marciano came into my view and stared him right in the eyes until he turned away from me. I wanted him to know that I knew what he had planned and I was not going to make earning that extra thousand dollars easy for him.

Watson and I walked to the center of the ring and waited for instructions from the referee. As always, I started talking trash and trying to intimidate my opponent before the bell rang. I would do this both to anger him and to take his mind off any plans he may have previously made before the match. This time, though, Marciano immediately jumped in between us as I slapped Watson with an open hand to the face. Rocky pushed us apart and started screaming at me to get back to my corner. When the bell rang, I was out of my corner and all over Watson, pushing him back in his corner and pounding on him as hard as I could, trying to end the match as quickly as possible. This was my chance at the big time, at the big money, and I wanted to get out of this match without an injury. The next thing I knew, Marciano had come up behind me and grabbed me by both arms and was pulling me back and away from Watson, but holding me long enough for Watson to catch me one good one on the jaw with a closed fist and knock me to the mat.

As I was getting up off the mat, trying to clear the cobwebs out of my head, Watson attacked me again, this time throwing me over the top rope onto the cement floor. Back in those days, any other referee would have disqualified Watson for such a move. Throwing a man over the top rope some twelve feet onto a bare cement floor can break bones. But Marciano pretended he did not see it. I climbed back into the ring and tried to complain to him, but Marciano just pushed me away. So again I attacked Watson, pushing him back into the corner so I could continue the pounding I had started earlier. However, just as I was gaining the upper hand, Marciano came up behind me for a second time, pulling and pushing me away from Watson. This again took my mind away from my opponent. When I turned away from Marciano, Watson again caught me flush on the jaw with a roundhouse right that almost knocked me out for the second time that night. I was so mad I was ready to spit bricks. I was starting not to care if I was disqualified for hitting the referee or not. I got off the mat and hit Watson as hard as I could with a straight right hand, knocking him to the mat. Then I turned my attention to Marciano. I grabbed a handful of what little hair Rocky had left and pulled his head down, then hit him as hard as I could in the back of the head with a closed fist. Marciano went down to the mat on one knee and I went back after Watson.

I was about to try for the Iron Claw when out of the corner of my eye I saw Marciano coming at me from behind. The boxing great hit me upside the head harder than I think I have ever been hit in my life, knocking me down but not out. At that point, Gene Kiniski—who had been watching the match from the crowd—jumped into the ring to try to even things out. Four Buffalo police officers immediately followed Gene into the ring, blackjacks in hand, trying to bring the match under control. I again went after Marciano but was cut short by Watson. The next thing I knew, Marciano called for the bell and disqualified me seventeen minutes and eleven seconds into the match because of Gene's interference.

I would not get another shot at the heavyweight title until almost a year later. On July 31, 1962, I defeated Vern Gagna in front of a sold-out crowd in Omaha, Nebraska, and won the AWA World Heavyweight Championship title in a very bloody match that lasted almost an hour. I was finally the world champion and the money was starting to come in, but I now had to travel more than ever to defend the title. I was getting calls from promoters all over the world who wanted to book me throughout the United States, Canada, and Mexico.

Less than a year later, while still the AWA world champion, I had another big match with Vern Gagna, who had just won the NWA World Heavyweight Championship title a few months earlier. This match was for both the AWA and the NWA title. On July 7, 1963, I defeated Gagna for the second time, uniting both titles in Omaha, Nebraska.

This should have been one of the happiest times in my life but I was still grieving for my son, Jack Jr. The main reason I had endured all the hard times was so one day I could give my family all the things every good father and husband wants for his family. What was the point of succeeding now that my son was gone? Almost two years had gone by, but little Jack Jr.'s death was still on my mind as if it had happened the day before. I even wondered if there was a God up there in heaven at times. If He did exist, how could He be so cruel as to take from me the most perfect thing in my life, a member of my precious family?

My doubts about God came to a head one night while driving home to our trailer near Niagara Falls after a match in Buffalo, New York. The weather was terrible. It had been snowing for days and the roads were extremely icy and slippery. I probably should have stayed in Buffalo until morning, but I wanted to be with my family. Doris was still having a tough time of it after Jack Jr.'s death. She did not talk about it but I could see the hurt on her face when I would come home after a week on the road. She had become withdrawn and I knew how much she blamed herself for what had happened. Seeing this hurt in my wife's eyes hurt me as much as my son's death.

I was driving over Peace Bridge in northern New York State when a large truck lost control and almost hit me. Just as I thought we were going to crash I screamed out, "Lord, if you are there please help my family and me get back to Texas. Help me get off the road and give my wife and remaining sons a good home to grow up in. If you will help me do this, Lord, I will serve you the best I can for the rest of my life." The truck barely missed hitting me, sending my car into the guardrail. As I got out of my car to inspect the damage, I started thinking about losing my son and how bad I felt inside. I looked up at the dark clouds above me on that cold New York evening as I stood in the middle of Peace Bridge and said, "Lord, I'm sorry, but I just do not think that you are out there."

Before the end of 1965, Doris and I had finally saved up enough money to get the family and our mobile home back to Texas. Earlier, I had been forced into vacating all my titles because of my refusal to travel and defend them. I was having masses of trouble with most all the promoters up north; seems my attitude had turned most of them against me. But I had gotten to the point where I did not care about the titles to begin with; I just did not want to leave my family alone while I traveled all over North America. So, after much thought, I decided the best thing for me to do was to quit the promoters I had been working for in New York and Canada due to the many disagreements we had over my matches. I packed all the family belongings in the car and we headed down to Corpus Christi to buy that bait and tackle shop we had talked about for so long. On our way to Corpus, we stayed with my parents in Dallas for a couple of weeks so they could get to know their three remaining grandchildren.

On the drive down to Texas, I began to try to put my career in perspective. I wanted to stay in the wrestling business because I had now invested so much time in the business that I did not know what I would do if I decided to give up on it. I was thinking that I could wrestle on weekends and fly in and out of Corpus, but I was not sure that's what I really wanted. I thought I would just wait and see how things turned out once we settled down. While we were at my parents' house, I learned that word had gotten around that I was home for good and all the local promoters in Texas were trying to get in touch with me.

One promoter tracked me down to my parents' house, banged on the door, and begged me for just a minute of my time. "Fritz, please take a moment to listen to what I have to say," he insisted. When I finally agreed to talk to him, he told me that wrestling was not doing well at all in Dallas, Fort Worth, and Houston. Ed McLemore was the area promoter and the crowds were dwindling down to nothing due to the lack of talent. Most of the big names were wrestling up north where the money and talent was. Doris and I talked it over and decided the best I could offer him was to wrestle part-time while living in Corpus and running our bait and tackle shop.

The next day we were getting the boys ready to leave when a phone call came in for me. It was Ed McLemore himself and he wanted to talk. I explained to Ed that we were on our way out of town but he insisted, saying he needed to talk to me right then and he could be at my parents' house in about thirty minutes. After thinking it over a few minutes, I told him he could come on out and we could talk. I told Doris that Ed McLemore was on his way over and I wanted to hear what he had to say before we left. When Ed arrived, we all sat down while he told Doris and me how sorry he was to learn about Jack Jr.'s death. Then he told me about his plan. Texas Championship Wrestling had a good TV show on Channel 4 in Dallas at the time, but they did not have any big stars. All the talent Ed was able to get together in Texas was just a few over-the-hill wrestlers. Ed thought that a big name like mine could make the show a hit, not to mention the crowds that would swarm to the arenas to see me and my now famous Iron Claw.

Ed made his pitch, so Doris and I talked it over and decided what the hell. The bait and tackle shop would have to wait. Ed and I made a very good deal that would let me wrestle in the Texas area and be close to my family. Ed and I agreed that if I would come and work with him, if he ever made the decision to leave the wrestling business I would have first option on any sale of the franchise. Therefore, two weeks later I started wrestling on Channel 4's *Studio Championship Wrestling*. Shortly after I joined the show, five other top stars quickly joined up. Things were going well, so Doris and I started making plans to move to Dallas and gave up on the bait and tackle shop once again. The kind of money that Ed had offered me took our minds off Corpus Christi.

It was around that time, after moving to Texas for good, that I decided to drop the German persona I had cultivated up north. I was rid of the fake German accent, the goose step, the marching boots, and red cape, but decided to keep the stage name of Fritz Von Erich because of the success and titles connected with that stage name. From that time on, I would enter the ring dressed in a simple black T-shirt and wrestling tights. There would be no more capes or fancy ring jackets; there would be no more fake German accents. I was just Fritz Von Erich from Jewett, Texas. I would later change my birthplace to Lake Dallas because of all my business connections in the Lake Dallas area.

I guess I wrestled on TV for close to two months before I returned to the ring at the Sportatorium after all the years up north. The first Friday night that I wrestled at the Sportatorium in Dallas they sold every seat, turning people away at the door. I never knew I had so many fans in the Dallas area and that warm greeting sure made me glad I was home. I won my match that night with the Iron Claw, and most of the fans in the building were cheering for me instead of booing me, which was something I would have to get used to now that I was home to stay. That night, Texas championship wrestling changed for years to come. All the big wrestling names from up north started turning up in Dallas, doing anything and everything they could to get booked to wrestle in the Texas area.

I started making more money than I ever had in my life. Since we were back in Texas, Doris and I were getting to know many of our old friends again, including some of my former classmates from SMU. I would later become partners with two of them in a real estate company called Lamberth and Forester, which specialized in joint venture in real estate investments. I started investing much of my own money in raw land. I have always liked the feeling of owning land. When I was growing up, my father used to say, "Jack, they're not making any more land, so when you get older and buy your own place, hold on to it." This was what I wanted for my family, our own land where my boys and I could hunt and fish while the property appreciated in value.

With the money we got for selling our mobile home and the money I was making in Dallas wrestling on Channel 4, we finally saved enough to pay cash for a real house in the Farmers Branch area of Dallas. It was located between Josey and Webb's Chapel Road and it was not just a trailer or some run-down apartment or motel room but a real house. The house was about sixteen hundred square feet; it was small, but it was the cutest little place and

Doris just fell in love with it. It was our family's first real home. I believe we paid right around eighteen thousand for the place.

The Sportatorium was only taking in about $150 to $200 per show before I arrived and my success as a box office draw made me a legend among the promoters in Texas, where the Sportatorium started taking in between fifteen and twenty-five hundred dollars per show, and was often times sold out. I had been back in Texas for less than a year when Ed McLemore started looking for larger arenas for the title matches; seems they were turning too many fans away at the Sportatorium due to not enough seating capacity. I was in demand everywhere. First, the Fort Worth people made me a very generous offer, then Morris Siegel in Houston—who was over his heart attack and doing well—made me an offer that made my mouth water. Even the people in San Antonio tried to cut a deal with me. It was hard to get used to being such a big success. Even though I had been in the wrestling business for a long time, my jump to stardom seemed like it happened overnight.

Our boys were growing fast, and before long we decided to find a larger home for our family of five. We had invested in some land, about 168 acres for less than five hundred dollars an acre just north of Lake Dallas in Denton County. Since both Doris and I were raised in the country, we both agreed that we wanted to raise our boys in a place where they could hunt, fish, and roam the countryside every day just as my Granddaddy Ross and I had done many times before in Jewett Texas.

My business ventures continued to do well. We all moved into a small house on the land we had purchased, the same house that I live in now, by the way. The family all lived here as Doris and I began to build our dream home. Doris designed it herself; she drew the plans on the back of a grocery sack from Piggy Wiggly one day while we were sitting under a tree on our new land, watching the boys running around in the woods. She soon transferred the drawings to some freezer wrap.

An architect friend of mine took the plans and tried to make copies, but the freezer wrap almost ruined his copy machine. We had our new house built in three stages. The finished product was a ranch-style brick home not far from Interstate 35E near Corinth, Texas. The land there was virgin wilderness and it was a perfect place for Doris and me to raise our family. Things could not have been better; we were settling down and I was, for the most part, at home with my family and not traveling around from place to place. Doris and I tried to stay busy in our new surroundings as we both tried to put Jack Jr.'s death behind us.

CHAPTER 5

In the years that followed, things were really starting to go my way. In fact, what I have always considered my biggest break came in December 1966, when I took my first tour overseas. Professional wrestling had started getting big all over the world. Promoters from Japan and parts of the Middle East were offering big money to all U.S. promotions to include them in a new annual world tour that was being put together back in the United States. The money I had been offered to make that trip to Japan and the Middle East was such that there was no way I could turn it down. It was this match that really made me a success all over the world. It was when I faced a Japanese wrestling legend known as "The Giant Baba."

I have always considered winning this match to be one of the biggest flukes that ever took place in my career. The Giant Baba was one of the best pro wrestlers in all of Japan. For a big man, his speed was matched by none. His experience in the ring was more than equal to that of my own. This match was to take place at the Nippon Budokan, a martial arts arena that was also used as a concert hall, located in Kitanomaru Park, Chiyoda Word, in Tokyo, Japan. When I walked into the arena early that morning before the match was to take place, there was no wrestling ring in sight. As I looked around, all I saw was a Japanese ring, which was octagonal in shape and had no ropes. But I did not care what the ring looked like. I was being paid good money to wrestle, and wrestle I did.

That night, as I exited my dressing room and made my way to the octagon-shaped wrestling ring, the crowd was silent. Japanese wrestling fans were so much different from their American counterparts back in the early days. They would sit in their seats very quietly, never booing or talking trash to wrestlers entering the ring. When the excitement of the matches would overcome them, they would occasionally slap the side of their leg with a hand fan that was intended to keep them cool, since the arena had no air-conditioning.

As I approached this Japanese ring that night, I noticed that two boxes about eighteen inches square and filled with some type of white powder had been placed in each of our corners. One of the Japanese referees met me before I stepped on the mat and began to motion for me to go the center of the ring. I was going to hold up my right arm and show the Japanese fans my Claw, but the referee kept tapping me on the shoulder, saying something in Japanese that was like none of the Japanese words that I had tried to learn before leaving the States. I tried to tell the little guy that I could not understand him, but he just kept tapping me on the shoulder and pointing to the center of the ring.

I gave up on making my grand appearance and headed for the center of the ring, where Baba and another referee stood staring at me with big smiles on their faces. The referee that was standing with Baba begins to motion him and I together with a hand gesture that I took to mean it was time to wrestle. Just as I was about to reach out and slap at my opponent, Baba held up his hand to the referee, turned and walked back to his corner and stepped into that box of powder, bent down and got some of the powder and began rubbing it on his hands as he stared at me with an even bigger smile on his face than the one he had as I entered the ring.

I looked at the referee standing beside me and tried my best to ask him what was going on. He just stood there looking at me and shaking his head as Baba returned to the center of the ring. I was still waving my arms in the air and pointing at Baba as I continued to try to find a way to tell the referee that I was not going to stand for any this. The referee continued to stand there and shake his head, trying his best not to burst out laughing. Then, the referee's hand goes up in the air and he started motioning Baba and I back together with more hand gestures. I again took this to mean that it was time to wrestle.

At this point I decided I would not try to slap Baba, so I crouched down, getting ready to jump out at him instead when the referee gave the word. Again, Baba raised his right hand in the air, took a step backward, turned and walked back to his corner. He stepped back into the square box, bent down and began rubbing his hands in the white powder for the second time. But this time, Baba almost burst out laughing and so did some of the fans sitting near ringside. I knew at this point that Baba was making his grand appearance at my cost and I was not going to let him get away with it. I stood back up and waited patiently for Baba to finish his grandstanding and get back to the center of the ring, where he nodded to the referee that he was now ready to begin. Just as the referee started to give the signal to begin, I held up my right hand and stepped backward, turned, and made my way back to my corner, where I stepped into my square box filled with my white powder. I then bent down and started rubbing power on my hands, then under my arms, and all over my chest.

This infuriated Baba. He started screaming at the referee as I stood in my corner and laughed at him. The referee, whose smile was gone, started motioning me back to the center ring with a flurry of wild hand gestures. As I returned to the center of the ring, I was dragging white power behind me, which was starting to coat the ring floor. Baba looked at the ring floor in horror, trying to get the referee's attention as he pointed at the mess I had made on the floor. About this time, I had arrived back at the center of the ring and was through joking around; it was now time to fight. I hit Baba with a roundhouse right that took him totally by surprise. I still had a handful of powder when I hit him, which caused a cloud of the white power to linger in the air as Baba was sent to the mat, dazed. I was not about to let this opportunity pass me by. I ran behind him and started to apply the sleeper hold to the throat of the Giant Baba. The referee at this time was more confused than Baba as he kept running around the two of us, not sure what he should do. Baba was almost unconscious in the center of the ring when I let him go. I did not want to win this match with a sleeper hold; it had to be with the Iron Claw.

I came out from behind Baba and jumped on top of him, applying the Claw to the top of his head as I began digging my fingernails into the sides of his face. My thumbnail was dug into the top of his eyebrow, which started blood flowing down his face. The Japanese fans were stunned and the whole arena was totally quiet; you really could have heard a pin drop. Baba made a desperate attempt to get to his feet, but the Claw had started cutting the flow of blood to the brain and he was paralyzed and helpless. The referee was trying to get me to let go so he could raise my arm in the air, letting everyone know that I was the victor.

On that night, December 3, 1966, I defeated The Giant Baba in just over three minutes and made wrestling history. No American had ever defeated this giant of a man and this match had been for the new, vacant NWA World International Heavyweight title. After I had won the match that night using the Iron Claw, the Japanese fans came unglued. I became an overnight success in Japan. A song was written about my Iron Claw and me and the Japanese fans even gave me a nickname—Tetsu no Tsume, which means "Nails of the Iron." After that match, I became the most famous gaijin (foreign) wrestler in all of Japan. Wrestling was becoming popular all over the world, and Texas wrestling was again on top.

When I got back to the States, the American fans who met me at the airport had even named a dance in my honor; they called it "the Claw." So all the work, the difficulties, the doing without, the many injuries I had endured all those years were paying off. I felt that I had finally made it to the top of my chosen profession.

Life at home was better than ever. The boys were all growing up so fast and Doris was always busy trying to keep track of them. I would try to spend all the time I could with my family. On our land there were wide-open spaces. Several ponds and creeks, and woods full of deer, squirrels, birds, and all sorts of other wildlife. I bought each of my boys a horse, a mini-bike, and a dog after returning from Japan. I also made them work their butts off for them.

I gave each one of the boys their respective chores, and let them know I fully expected each of them to do the best they could. I wanted them to understand that you had to work hard in this world if you wanted to have nice things.

We started raising quail at our ranch on Lake Dallas, and at any given time we had five hundred to one thousand of them. The boys would feed and water all the quails; they cleaned their cages, even put the eggs in the incubator and hatched them. In my opinion, that is the way all kids in the world should grow up, living out in the country and learning about hard work and its rewards. The values that children learn from being in the country are well worth the parents trying to get them out there. Unfortunately, the way the population keeps getting larger and larger, soon there will not be any wilderness left for kids to play in.

Chores for the boys were listed on a yellow notepad divided into three sections that I kept hung up in the garage. Kevin's job every day was to make sure the quail pens and the garage stayed cleaned, and on some days he would take care of all the dogs also.

I always gave David the most important jobs because I felt he was more responsible than Kevin and Kerry. Therefore, when something needed doing I would always tell David, who in turn would always make Kevin or Kerry do it, which would usually end in a fight between the three of them.

With us living on that ranch out in the country the boys had plenty of work to do, but sometimes they would try everything possible to get out of their assigned chores. When company came over, they would splash water all over their faces to look like they were tired and sweating, and then ask our visitors to please go and ask Dad if they could stop working for a while because they were so tired. Most of the time, our company would come into the house and try to convince us to give the boys a break. Doris and I were wise to their little tricks, but there were a few times that I think those boys convinced some of our friends that Doris and I were a couple of slave drivers.

Since Kevin was the oldest, he did everything first to make sure it was safe for his younger brothers. Whether it was climbing a tree or swimming in a creek, I always told Kevin to look after his little brothers, and if anything happened to them, it had better happen to him first. Kevin did a very good job of taking care of his brothers. The three of them were all close in age and the best of friends.

Most days they were out in the woods from sunup to sundown. At times, Doris and I had a hard time keeping track of them. We would always know that they were somewhere out there on the 150 acres, but the question was, where? Just about all of their childhood games took place out there on that ranch. And the three of them loved every minute of growing up in the country.

Growing up, those boys had eight Labrador retrievers, all purebred and very valuable dogs. It seems like one of those dogs was always having puppies. At times, we had so many dogs that I could not give them away fast enough.

The best all-around dog I ever had was one I named Tugboat. I had old Tugboat so well trained that he would fetch the morning paper on voice command, over the house inter-\com. That dog would even bring us fresh eggs from the chicken house each morning, and I never saw him break or even crack a single one.

Tugboat knew each of my boys by name, and he would go to the boy whose name was called. One day when I came home from work, Doris told me that she had been looking for Kerry earlier that day and could not find him, so she called for Tugboat to find him. Tug circled the house and then went back to his doghouse, so Doris called him back and told him to try again. Again, Tug circled the house and ran back to his doghouse. Finally, Doris went over to the doghouse to drag Tug out for another try and there, next to old Tugboat, was Kerry, sound asleep. I later became one of the founders of the North Texas Retriever Club. I have seen many a fine dog in my time, but in my opinion, old Tugboat was the smartest dog I have ever had the pleasure of rising.

One thing that I thought was somewhat funny was the fact that my real name was Jack Adkisson, but everyone called me Fritz or Mr. Von Erich. I always worried that my stage name might confuse the boys, but I don't think it ever did. They really thought all families were like that. When Kerry was very young, I heard him ask one of his friends one day what his father's other name was.

Another funny story about the three oldest boys when they were growing up centered around a broken window. Seems one day a window came up broken at the house and nobody knew who had broken it. However, Doris and I knew that two of the boys were covering for the third. I called all three boys into the living room, asking them how the window got broken. Each boy looked at one another then back at me and said they had no idea.

Since Kevin was the oldest, I told him to go and get my belt out of my closet and bring it to me. Kevin looked at me with wide eyes. I told the boys that I knew one of them had broken the window and since none of the three was man enough to admit his mistake, I was going to have to spank all of them. I lined them up and was just about to spank David first when he turned to me and said quietly, "Uh, Dad? Would you mind if Kevin, Kerry, and I had a few minutes alone, please?" I said sure, and left the room.

Soon, Kerry came to me with tears in his eyes. "Dad, I'm the one who broke the window," he said. I decided not to spank Kerry that night, but instead called all three boys back in the room and told them that sometimes we all do things that we regret. A real man should not be ashamed to admit he made a mistake, and should always try to learn from that mistake so it does not happen again.

Doris had become a very devoted Christian by this time, I think mostly because of the deaths of her brother and Jack Jr. She would take the boys to church every Sunday morning, but I would never go with them. I just really did not believe in anything at the time. My mother had been a very religious person and made me go to church every Sunday when I was growing up, but I had later stopped when I left home for college. Besides, I felt I did not have time for something like that.

Doris would tell the boys that if they believed in the Lord Jesus Christ, they had to believe in the devil. She would tell them all kinds of stories about the mean old devil. I did not want my boys having nightmares about Satan and waking up scared in the middle of the night, so I would go in their room after Doris left and joke with them. I would say, "Look, guys, hey, I do not want you boys to worry about that kind of stuff. If there is a Hell, and if there really is an old devil, your dad will go on ahead of you. When I get to Hell, which is where your mother thinks I am going anyway, I will take that place over and I will dropkick that devil. I will body slam him and then, I will finish him off by putting the Iron Claw on him, right there in front of the rest of my friends (who should all be there when I get there) and when you guys get down there too, I will be the one in charge." The boys would laugh and later they would fall sound asleep. I just did not want to see them frightened. A dark room can be a scary place for a little boy. I guess I realize now what I did for those boys was a stupid thing. I guess all children should learn to be scared of Satan, but at the time, my mind was still not yet made up to the fact that God was even out there.

One day, some very close friends of ours, Herschel and Sally Forester, invited us to go to a revival at the First Baptist Church in Dallas to hear Dr. W. A. Criswell. I did not really want to go, but I got along so well with Herschel and Sally and enjoyed their company so much that I felt that I would hurt their feelings if I stayed home. That was the only reason I went that morning. Once I got sat down in church and started listening to what was being said, I found myself very moved by Dr. Criswell's sermon. The next thing I remember is finding myself at altar call, going forward with tears in my eyes. I will never forget what I told Dr. Criswell just after I committed my life to the Lord. It was a very emotional moment, and I told him, "Dr. Criswell, you are the best damn preacher I have ever heard in my life."

I was having quite a bit of material success at the time and I thought I was a smart person. As time went on, I found that I had been thinking more of my success and less and less of the Lord. Then, I guess it was around 1974 or '75, I started having major business problems. I had tried to move too far too fast and things were not working out. I was having problems at night trying to sleep, I was not eating right, and I was just plain forgetting about my family. Moreover, my body felt as though it was falling apart. I hurt all over most of the time because of all the wrestling injuries I had suffered over the years.

One morning, I woke up and my problems seemed to be much worse than the day before. I had a ringing in my ears and could barely hear; I sensed a voice in my head that kept repeating over and over, "Psalms 23, Psalms 23…"

I had no idea what Psalms 23 was. All I knew was that it was a passage from the Bible, so I started looking around for Doris's Bible so I could look it up. When I found the Book of Psalms and started reading Psalms 23, I felt a chill run up and down my spine as the words seemed to jump out at me and tears clouded my eyes as I read the following passage:

The lord is my shepherd;
I shall not want.
He makes me lie down in green pastures:
He leads me besides the still waters.
He restoreth my soul:
He leadeth me in the path of righteousness
For his name's sake
Yea, though I shall walk through the valley of the shadow of death,

I will fear no evil:
For Thou are with me;
Thy rod and Thy staff will comfort me.
Thou preparest a table before me, in the presence of my enemies;
Thou anointest my head with oil
My cup runneth over.
Surely, goodness and mercy shall follow me for the rest of my life
And I will dwell in the house of the Lord forever.

The more I thought of this simple verse, the more I felt chills. The truth was the words in Psalms 23 were the answers to all my problems. From that time forward, I turned my problems over to the Lord. After that, they were all straightened out.

Not long after that day I was driving down I-35E on my way to the Sportatorium in very heavy traffic when a strange feeling came over me. I pulled my car over to the side of the road, turned the engine off, and just sat there in a sort of a trance. All kinds of strange thoughts were running through my head and I began to hear someone talking to me. It was not a voice, but it was as clear as the words on this page. It said, "What was it you asked me for? And where are you now? And what did you promise me?"

I then started to recall that night up north standing in the middle of Peace Bridge shortly after I had lost my oldest son. I had made a promise by saying, "Lord, if you will just help me, I will serve you for the rest of my life." It had taken me a while to start living up to my end of the bargain, but I was finally ready to begin. I guess I am still stumbling along now after all these years, even with death getting closer and closer for me, and I am not sure that I ever did what I promised the Lord that I would do. The deal I had made with the Lord up north that evening was that if He would help me get my family back to Texas—where I could support them and raise my boys in a home instead of a trailer house or a motel room—I would serve the Lord for the rest of my life. He had kept his promise to me, and now I had to keep my promise to him. So I put my head on the steering wheel and closed my eyes and told the Lord that I now knew He was there and I had stumbled along in my life and might keep on stumbling but I would never let go of his hand.

Since that morning, all my boys became born-again Christians. We all agreed that it was Doris who had been the spiritual inspiration for the Adkisson family. All those boys loved their mother so much. I always knew that if it had not been for her, I would have never made it to the top of my field. She was always there for the boys and me even though sometimes I did not pay enough attention to the things she said. Even now, after all the bad things that happened to our family, I still love that woman. And I guess I will love her until the day I die.

CHAPTER 6

In 1965, Doris again found herself expecting another baby. And again we were both hoping for a little girl. We would tell each other and the boys to "think PINK," and we convinced ourselves that this time we were going to add a girl to the Adkisson family. Doris and her friends were even out shopping for clothes for our new daughter. Well, I guess high hopes don't count for much, because on March 2, 1966, in Denton County, Texas, Doris gave birth to our fifth son, a very healthy boy we named Michael Brett Adkisson.

When Mike was born the older boys were already in Little League athletics going out for track, football, baseball, and basketball. Doris and I would encourage all the boys to go out for sports, but we never tried to push them into doing something just because the other boys were doing it. If they did not enjoy it or did not want to do it, they did not have to.

Kevin, David, and Kerry were all close in age, so they were always playing games with each other. All the kids around the Lake Dallas area were invited to come over and play with the boys anytime they wanted to get a game started. It seems like most times there would be at least eight to ten kids hanging around our house all the time. If I was not busy, I would referee a baseball or football game and Doris would always come up with refreshments and healthy snacks for everyone. Sometimes Doris and I would even get out there and play when there were not enough kids around to have a team.

When the boys started junior high school, they began to mature both physically and mentally. They were at that age where I thought they would benefit from working out with weights, so Doris and I would try very hard to encourage them to train their muscles. I went out and purchased all kinds of fancy gym equipment for the three of them. Then, one evening, I somehow managed to get all the boys together in one room and showed them how to use everything. After a while I left them alone to work out by themselves, but every now and then I would sneak a peek to see how they were doing. More often than not they were just horsing around. They would all later complain that weight training was too hard and made them sore all over.

That attitude would later change somewhat after one of the most popular girls in school commented on Kevin's muscles and wanted to know if he worked out. Kevin came home and started working out that very same day. From then on he worked out every day after school and would be waiting for me when I got home in the evenings to ask me all kinds of questions about how to build up this muscle or that muscle. The next thing I knew, all three of the boys started hitting the weights every evening. They would later all become very dedicated weightlifters as the three of them grew older.

Kevin, David, and Kerry were very good to their little brother Mike, unlike some boys who feel their little brother is a pain in the ass. They were always playing games with Mike and trying to teach him things that were passed down from me to Kevin and from Kevin to David and right on down the line. Of course there would be times Doris and I had to get on the older boys for trying to teach Mike things he was too young to learn. They wanted him to be able to play games and lift weights with them right away, but he was much too young at that time. Sometimes I had to spank their butts for picking on the little guy. I think that Kerry got in the most trouble for picking on Mike, partly because he was so happy that he was no longer the baby in the family.

Less than four years after Mike was born, Doris came up pregnant again. This time no one in our family was allowed to mention anything about a little girl, or the color pink. The whole family just assumed that it would be a boy, but I could tell that in the back of Doris's mind she was still hoping for that little girl whom she had already named Jill back years ago. In the back of my mind, I was thinking about starting my own ball team.

On September 30, 1969, in Denton, Doris gave birth to our sixth son, Chris Barton Adkisson. The night Chris was born I was still the top wrestler in the Texas area and was scheduled to be in the main event at the Sportatorium against Johnny "The Hammer" Valentine. That night at the Sportatorium the announcer got on the loudspeaker and told the fans that Doris and I would be having a new addition to our family that night. The fans were told that I would still wrestle in the main event after the baby was born, no matter what time it was. Sure enough, Chris was born shortly before midnight, and as soon as I knew Doris and the baby were doing fine, I kissed Doris, put the boys in the car, and took off to Dallas changing into my wrestling tights in the car. I was now ready to kick The Hammer's butt. We arrived at the Sportatorium at twelve-thirty in the morning and I don't think any of the fans had even left. The announcers had told the crowd that Doris and I had a new baby boy we named Chris Barton Adkisson. When I walked out to the ring early that morning, the crowd just about blew the ceiling off the Sportatorium.

It would be hard for me to tell you how great I felt that night. Fans came rushing up to the ring to shake my hand. When I finally got to the dressing room and finished my shower, got dressed, rounded up the boys, and headed out the door to the car, fans were waiting outside in the parking lot to congratulate me on the newest addition to our family. I won the match that night just for Doris and my new son, Chris. Even now I am convinced that Johnny Valentine did not hand me that match as a present.

I have often been asked who was the best wrestler I ever faced in my career, and who was the meanest. It would be hard for me to say who the greatest wrestler I ever stepped into the ring with was because I have seen so many great wrestlers in my time. But believe me, Johnny Valentine was one of the meanest!

Johnny and I went back to my younger years, when I was just getting started in the business up north and traveling around Canada. Johnny already had many fans in the Canadian area and was wrestling in main events when I arrived on the scene in Edmonton. The two of us never got along that well. I guess I always considered Johnny sort of a psycho. He was always getting disqualified for one thing or another and was known to get a little too carried away and attack fans at ringside that did not see things his way. Johnny followed me to Texas soon after I left New York and settled in Dallas. He and I would go on to beat on each other senselessly night after night, drawing sold-out crowds wherever we would wrestle. That night in Dallas when Chris was born, Johnny and I were both covered in blood after the match. As I was trying to make my way back to the dressing room, I remember hearing Johnny on the loudspeaker telling the crowd after the match that he could not believe another Von Erich boy had hatched!

The wrestling fans in Dallas were the best fans I ever had. I loved every one of them and I never complained about signing autographs because I knew my fans were the reason I was in such demand. I always did my best to give those fans one hundred and ten percent, and I would later try my best to pass this love for the fans on to my boys.

If ever there was moment that was a turning point for the boys and their attitudes it was when Kevin was a freshman in high school. One of the seniors in the school was picking on him. It was simply an unfortunate circumstance and it probably came with the territory of having a famous father who was a big tough professional wrestler.

Doris knew something was bothering Kevin that day when he came home for school. She started asking him questions about why he was acting so strange and didn't want to talk to anyone. It was David who later told her about the older boy picking on Kevin in front of him and the other kids. The older boy had been calling Kevin names and trying to get him in a fight, saying that he was a pansy like his old man. Doris took his concerns seriously and called me at work, saying it was very important that I come home early that night to talk with Kevin.

When I arrived home that evening, Kevin relayed to me what was going on in school. After asking Kevin a few questions and thinking about his situation, I told him the same thing I had told Jack Jr. about fifteen years earlier. Stand up to the bullies of the world or they will never respect you. You can expect the same treatment from them every day until you do stand up to them. And after you stand up to them, things will change.

Back in 1958, when a bully had pushed Jack Jr. off his bike, Doris had told Jack Jr. to tell the bully's mother what had happened. When I found out what she had told our son, I hit the roof. "You have ruined our son," I told her; "I will not bring our boy up to be a tattletale; he must learn to handle things himself." Then I took little Jack Jr. for a walk and tried to explain to him that he would encounter bullies of all types for the rest of his life and he had to learn how to take care of things on his own. "The next time he pushes you around, you punch that bully in the nose as hard as you can," I said. A few weeks later, I came home and Doris told me that Jack Jr. had taken my advice. When the trailer-court bully tried to take his bike, Jack Jr. hauled off and hit that kid in the nose as hard as he could, sending the other boy running home crying.

Kevin's problem was a little different because the eyes of the school were on him. The kid who was beating up on him was the king of all the bullies. He was bigger, stronger, and three years older than Kevin. All the kids in school were having problems with this guy and they were hoping Kevin would be the one to stop him. I guess all the other kids felt like since Kevin's father was a big wrestler, this had to make Kevin a tough guy also.

I could tell after talking to Kevin that evening that this confrontation was very important to him. Therefore, Kevin and I went for a walk. "When that bully starts that crap with you, I want you to stand up to him this time and kick him as hard as you can between the legs," I said. "Then start pounding on him and do not stop pounding on him until you know the fight is over.

"It is okay to be afraid, son," I told Kevin. "Fear is something that all of us feel in the pit of our stomachs when things happen that we are uncertain of. You will feel this fear in every unknown situation you face in your life up to the day that you die, so you have to get used to fear always being around. Learn to set it aside until what needs to be done gets done."

The next day, that same person walked up to Kevin and started the same thing all over again. This time, though, little Kevin turned into a wild man. Kevin kicked the guy right between the legs just as I had told him to do. When the guy fell to the ground, Kevin was on top of him, pounding him in the face. The bully got to his feet and grabbed Kevin in a headlock but let go after Kevin almost bit his finger off. Even after the bully let go, Kevin kept pounding on him as hard as he could. The school coaches finally pulled the two of them apart. The bully said he would quit if Kevin would quit, so Kevin tore back into him some more and the coaches had to pull them apart again. This time the coaches put boxing gloves on the two of them and Kevin beat that bully some more until the guy finally quit.

Things seemed to change around Lake Dallas High School after that. Nobody picked on Kevin Adkisson anymore. Even though he was a shy kid, he suddenly became very popular because he had done what so many of the other kids wanted to do. The bully of the school later became one of Kevin's best friends, because the guy respected him. All the girls took notice, too.

That was the turning point not just for Kevin but for the other three boys as well. After Kevin confronted that bully, all four of my sons developed positive attitudes about competition and standing up for what they believed was right. Since Kevin, who was the oldest of the brothers, had proven himself to all the other kids in school, David and Kerry was automatically proven also. Their newfound confidence made them work out harder, which in turn made them better athletes.

Lake Dallas High School, like most Texas schools in the seventies, did not have a real wrestling program. The school did try to put one together one year, but it never got off the ground. Therefore, instead of wrestling, the boys participated in football, basketball, and other sports. In addition, they excelled.

Kevin became the first All-State football player from his school. David became the second All-State athlete from Lake Dallas in both football and basketball. Kerry became the third. Kerry was All-State in football and named to the All-State and All-American Track Team. He also set the Texas state record for throwing the discus.

As far as I know, Kerry still holds that state high school record. In his senior year, he was so far ahead of the competition that in one track meet in one day he officially set new state records six times in six consecutive throws. When I was at SMU, I considered myself the best discus thrower in the state, but Kerry was better; he was a natural. Kerry asked me to coach him in discus throwing one year in high school. He knew I still held a few discus records at SMU, so he told me that if I would coach him, he could beat my record.

When I came home in the evening, Kerry and I would go to the discus ring we had put in next to our house. Kerry would throw and throw, I would film it, and we then would go watch the film. After that, we would go back out and throw some more. Kerry would study the films when he came home from school. This went on for a few years, until one day he broke the junior world record in college at the University of Houston.

The proudest I have ever seen that boy was when he broke the Southern Methodist school record at a Southwest Conference track meet. An old SMU track star named Jack Adkisson had held that discus record for over twenty years. For about the last three years, Kerry had been telling me he was going to break my record, and I guess he was true to his word.

While Kerry was a student at the University of Houston, he came home one day and said, "Dad, guess what? I am going for the gold." His dream had come true! He was going to represent the United States of America in the Moscow Olympic Games. However, our president at the time was Jimmy Carter, and due to a bunch of political bull, President Carter ordered the United States Olympic teams to boycott the games. I have always thought that was the dumbest thing a Unitesd States president could do. It was not fair to our boys; they had worked their butts off to get ready for those games, only to be let down by their own country.

Less than a year later, Kevin—who was in his last year of college—received an offer to play football for the Dallas Cowboys. I have never seen any boy so proud of what he had achieved in football as Kevin. He had gotten his picture in the *Dallas Morning News* showing him with the Cowboys staff as he looked over a contract that would be his after he graduated from North Texas State that year.

However, the deal fell apart after Kevin hurt his knee before the end of the year. He had to undergo reconstructive knee surgery and the Cowboys said they would not be able to use him with such a bad knee. There had been only three games left in the season when he hurt his knee and I felt so sorry for Kevin; playing pro football had been his dream. As with me, Kevin's pro football career ended with a knee injury. However, Kevin's injury was much worse than mine had been. All three of my oldest boys were just like their dad, wanting to play football or track more than anything, only to have some injury or turn of events stand in their way. Eventually, all three boys turned to wrestling. As everybody now knows, all three became superstars.

When the boys were not lifting weights, they were playing around the ranch. They had a football field they had made themselves that purposely had two trees in the middle of the playing field. One day I offered to have those two trees removed for them but they said no, it made playing football more challenging. One day, Kevin tackled Kerry, slamming him into one of the two trees and putting him in the hospital for a week during the Christmas holidays. Another time, a sharp broken tree branch went all the way through David's arm after he jumped up for a pass and landed in the tree. Kevin and Kerry had to pull him and his arm out of the tree and take him back to the house. Doris took him to the hospital, where he received twenty-six stitches in his arm.

I was always working with the boys, showing them that with the right attitude they could become champions at whatever activity or sport they wanted. Doris was the kind of mother who went to every game, cheering her boys on to do their best. She was more than a mother to those boys; she was their best friend.

The boys earned an allowance if they stuck to their chores and bodybuilding routines. David found it the hardest to stay disciplined while Kevin and Kerry did just fine. We would later have an entire gym built on our property along with a professional wrestling ring. I would have professional wrestlers and weight trainers come in and coach the boys every chance I could.

Kozrow Vaziri, better known as "The Iron Sheik," came out to the ranch many times to teach the boys wrestling and self-defense. Kozrow was a true champion. He won a gold medal for his native Iran wrestling at the 1968 Olympics games in Mexico City, and placed third in the 1969 World Cup competition. Before defecting to the United States, he was a bodyguard to the Peacock Throne in Iran. In 1972 and 1976 he worked as an assistant coach for the United States Olympic wrestling team. At the 1972 Olympic trials, Vern Gange discovered Kozrow and became his trainer; Gange would later give him his start in professional wrestling.

Kozrow made his wrestling debut in 1979 for the Worldwide Wrestling Federation (WWF). At first, he toured with the WWF under the name "The Great Hossein" and was introduced to the fans along with his manager, "Ayatollah Basie." When the Iranian hostage crisis began, Hossein and his manager became the most hated team in wrestling.

Kozrow's matches were classics in the art of wrestling. In the course of a single match, it was not at all unusual to see four or five variations of the suplex used by Kozrow. He was a man who could scientifically wrestle with anyone, yet was also a great brawler. On several occasions I had the privilege of watching Kozrow work out with his Iranian clubs. Those two clubs weighed seventy-five pounds each and he would twirl them behind his head in a way that seemed to defy the laws of gravity. There has been no one to this day that I know of—in or out of the ring—who has matched Kozrow's challenge to duplicate his repetitions with the Iranian clubs.

In 1983, Kozrow returned to the WWF wrestling under the name "The Iron Sheik" and challenging Bob Backlund, who had been the WWF world heavyweight champion for the previous five-and-a-half years. During the Iranian Club Challenge, broadcast on TV, the Sheik attacked Backlund and injured his left shoulder and arm. Soon after that, on December 26, 1983, the Sheik defeated the world champion with his dreaded "Camel Clutch Submission Hold" and put the wrestling world in a state of shock.

My boys all admired Kozrow and learned a lot about wrestling from him. He would remain a good friend to the Von Erich family for many years and play a big part in my sons' wrestling abilities.

When Kevin, David, and Kerry first started pro-wrestling together as a tag team, they were the first athletes to come out of the dressing room on their way to the ring with a song playing in the background. I am not sure which one of the boys had suggested it, but the song, if you remember, was "LaGrange" by ZZ Top. Now all the athletes at wrestling and boxing matches have their own personal songs.

When Mike and Chris were growing up, their heroes were their older brothers. Those two boys wanted to be just like their bothers more than anything. Mike was a great all-around athlete, which I thought meant that he took after Kevin. Mike holds the second best record in Lake Dallas for the best All-Around Athlete with forty-three points out of a possible fifty points; Kevin is first with forty-eight points.

Mike was one of those athletes who had bad luck when it came to injuries. It seemed to run in our family. He had a bad shoulder that stayed injured much of the time in high school football. However, Mike would insist on playing even with his bad shoulder. To him, sitting on the bench was not an option. In track he was an All-District hurdler, long jumper, and discus thrower. He placed second in district in the high jump and first on the sprint relay team.

Chris was the youngest of the boys, and because of asthma problems from early childhood he was somewhat behind his brothers in athletics. He tried so hard to be like the other boys and not let his asthma stand in the way, but he was sick throughout much of his youth. The medicine he took for asthma made his bones very brittle, and he had many broken bones when he was growing up. Still, he tried as hard as he could to be like Mike, who was trying to be like Kerry, and right on up the line.

Then came the time Chris wanted to try out for amateur wrestling. Doris and I were not too thrilled about it, but there was no stopping him. He was determined to be a wrestler, just like his father and three brothers. Once Chris had made up his mind, the family stood behind him and gave all the support we could. Chris won his first amateur wrestling match at the age of six.Looking back on my life now, I realize that my fans watched those boys grow up on national television and at the Sportatorium. The boys would insist on coming to the matches with me and many times I would have them at my side while I was being interviewed at ringside.

When Kevin was about fourteen and Kerry was ten or so, I was in a match with one of Playboy Gary Hart's boys. Hart, who managed several wrestlers at a time, always made a habit of being at ringside with his wrestlers. He would interfere with matches both for show and to give his boys an edge. One night while I was in a match with one of his wrestlers, Gary jumped in the ring to help his man, hitting me in the back of the head with some object he had picked up off the floor. Then both he and his man got me over in their corner and started beating up on me. Hart would pass a foreign object to his man and then distract the referee while his man worked me over with it.

The next thing I knew, I am on the mat trying to wipe the blood out of my eyes when Kevin and Kerry come jumping in the ring to try to help their old dad. It was a very stupid thing to do. Little Kerry picked up a bucket from beneath the ring apron, climbed in the ring with it, and threw it at Gary Hart, hitting him in the head; at the same time, Kevin ran up and started kicking Hart as hard as he could on the leg. I almost had a heart attack when I saw my two boys in the ring.

I was barely able to get up and get them out of the ring before Hart and his boy went after them. I was disqualified that night for outside interference and was not too sure how to handle the boys over the incident. They loved their dad and did not want to see me hurt. When we got home that night and Doris found out what had happened, I thought that woman was going to go through the roof. She jumped all over me, Kevin, and Kerry, giving us the lecture of our lives. Then she put her foot down, saying that from then on when the boys went to the matches with me they had to watch from the press box, which was above the wrestler's dressing room at the Sportatorium and well away from the action.

Doris was about the only person I knew of that I would not want to step into a ring with. She had a temper that was unmatched by all of us. When she put her foot down in our family, her word became law. All the boys, including me, were well aware of this.

When the boys were younger, if they got in fights with each other and Doris was around, she would walk away, ignore them, or just referee the fight. One time when a fight broke out in the house between two of the boys in front of Doris, she jumped in the middle of the boys and yelled, "If you boys are going to kill yourselves, then take it outside. I will not let you tear up my house."

If I could do one thing over in my life it would be to raise my boys again. I have so many fond memories of all of them growing up. Each one could be the nicest kid there was, and then the next minute he would do a 180-degree turnaround and give me and his mother more hell in five minutes than some parents see in a lifetime.

None of my boys were perfect. They all made mistakes like every other kid in the world. But! The one thing my boys had in common with each other was heart. I saw that in each one of those boys as they grew up. They all had a lot of heart.

CHAPTER 7

As the years passed by, I found that I was not only enjoying great success in the ring but I had developed a talent for promoting as well. With all the contacts I had made up north, I started bringing in the biggest wrestling talent from all over the world. *World Class Championship Wrestling* was holding the number one spot in the ratings. We were beating out other wrestling television shows by a rather large margin. I had also become a very good businessperson by this time and was doing business in parts of the world and places in the Middle East that were experiencing American-style wrestling for the very first time. Things could not have been going better for me and my family; my sons were doing very well in school and I had plenty of time to spend watching them grow into fine, healthy young men. I felt on top of the world.

I had found that with the Lord on my side, and with a lot of praying, my life began to take on a completely new meaning. My success grew more and more with each passing year. I was putting on charity events all over the country and giving a percentage of my earnings to the church and the community. All the big names in wrestling were trying to get into Texas, names like Dory Funk Sr. and Dory Funk Jr., who at the time was the National Wrestling Alliance's world champion. Also at the time, little brother Terry Funk was coming onto the wrestling scene. The eyes of the wrestling world were on World Class Wrestling and Dallas, Texas.

I would like to say a few words about the late Mr. Dory Funk Sr., who passed away of a heart attack back in 1973 doing what he loved the most. I had known old Dory for a few years; when we first met he was the superintendent at Cal Farley's Boys' Ranch outside Amarillo, where he had started a wrestling program for the kids. Shortly afterward, Dory would become the wrestling promoter in Amarillo, Texas, where he and I got to know each other very well. I had once heard that when attendance was down at the local wrestling matches there in Amarillo, Dory Sr. would jump in his truck and drive to all the bars around town taking on all comers and telling everyone they had better get their butts to the arena. Attendance would climb for a few weeks and then start dropping back again. So off to the bars he would go. Dory Sr. was not a physically large man, but he was a mean one. He and I had some bloody matches back in the late sixties and early seventies before he passed away, drawing record crowds to the local arenas.

We once had a hell of a match there in Amarillo. It was our first time wrestling together and my first match in Amarillo. When I arrived at the arena that evening the promoter told me the match that night would be a "special match," a one-fall—a no-time-limit, no-disqualification match, and falls would count outside the ring. This was something new to me; I had never heard of anything remotely like this at the time and was very skeptical. I looked at the promoter in disbelief. "No time limit! No disqualification!" I exclaimed. "Do you mean we could be here wrestling all night?"

"Until one of you pins the other," he replied calmly. I began to wonder what I had gotten myself into and who had thought this kind of match up. I did not like the sound of this at all because of the chance Dory and I would be taking. This kind of match could leave one of us or both of us injured and unable to wrestle for months. I knew deep down inside that it was going to be one hell of a match.

That night before the match started, I walked out of my dressing room to see how large the crowd was. When I opened the door, I could not believe my eyes. The arena was packed and fans were standing against the walls waiting for the main event to start. As I scanned the arena, there was not one place in that building that another fan could squeeze into. As I walked to the ring that night, the Amarillo fans booed and threw ice and wads of paper at me, something I was not used to since returning home to Texas. Dory made his appearance next and the fans screamed and cheered so loudly I thought my eardrums would explode. When the match did start, Dory and I were fighting in the ring, outside the ring, and then in the crowd, where some of the fans got carried away and tried to kick me. Security had surrounded us, trying to keep the fans out of the action the best they could. We were hitting each other with the metal ringside chairs or anything else we could get our hands on, trying to pin each other on the floor, on top of tables, or anywhere else to get the match over with. Later in the match we even broke through the side exit door that led outside behind the arena where the VIP parking lot was. Dory and I were just outside the exit door, standing toe to toe, going at it when Dory picked me up and body slammed me on the hood of the mayor's car, shattering the windshield and putting a large dent in the hood. That man did not know the meaning of the word quit. All the fans were pushing and shoving each other, trying to get a peek out the door to see who was winning.

Security had their hands full trying to hold the crowd back and screaming at the referee to get us back in the building. After about five minutes of fighting outside, under and on top of almost every car in that parking lot, the referee finally managed to get us back inside the building. The match continued for another forty minutes before I was able to get my hands on one of the metal ringside chairs and hit Dory Sr. in the back of the head, knocking him down long enough to get the Iron Claw on him and get a three-count from the referee.

That no-time-limit match lasted almost two hours and not one fan left the arena before the end of the match. When that match did end that night, Dory Sr. and I were both covered in blood. The skin on our backs and knees had been torn off from wrestling on the ground outside the arena. The security guards (who were off-duty Amarillo Police Officers) had to escort me back to my dressing room because of the drunken Amarillo fans who could not stand to see their hometown hero lose a wrestling match.

Later that night in my dressing room, while I was trying to get dressed as fast as possible and get to my private plane so I could get out of Amarillo, a police officer showed up in my dressing room. The officer told me I would have to pay for the damage that I had done to the mayor's car before I left Amarillo, or he would have to take me to jail. Everyone in the arena that night was a Dory Funk Sr. fan, and for a while there I was thinking this joker was really going to take me to jail. I tried to explain to him that he should be talking to Dory and not me. I mean after all, Dory slammed me down on the hood of the car; it was not as if I had a choice in the matter.

Then a few minutes later in walked old Dory Sr., who asked the officer what was going on. The police officer explained to Dory that the mayor was very upset over his windshield being broken out and had ask him to find out who was going to pay for the damage to his car. Dory looked over at me and smiled, then told the officer that the promotions people would take care of any damage to the mayor's car, and he needed to get his ass out of the wrestler's dressing room and go take care of the traffic. Dory then turned to me and said that he was going to drive me to the Amarillo airport because of the drunken fans who were still hanging around outside the arena.

After that first match in Amarillo, Dory Sr. and I became the best of friends. As it turned out, Dory was the person responsible for putting together that sold-out match that night. He and I would later come up with all kinds of matches with lots of crazy rules and names that sold out arenas all over the world. The Texas Death Match was one of the most popular of these special events. This wrestling match would take place in a steel cage that is lowered down over the entire ring itself.

The cage has only one door, which was locked at the beginning of the match with a padlock. This match, too, was a no-time-limit and no-disqualification match. A Texas Death Match would not end until one man could no longer continue, and the fans loved them. All the promoters overseas were begging us to bring them to their arenas.

This type of match became so popular that we later came up with another version called the Texas Barbed Wire Match. Barbed wire was strung all around the ring and ropes and the wrestlers would try to throw each other into the ropes while avoiding the same fate for themselves. The truth was, the barbed wire left many cuts that bled like crazy, but the scratches were not serious at all as long as the wrestlers could kept their face away from the barbed wire. It looked a lot worse than it really was. However, for days afterward the two men would look as though a wild cat had gotten hold of them. The money they would get for such an event had them all lined up at my door trying to get in on these wild, crazy matches.

The crowds loved all the new events we had started bringing into the arenas. Wrestling was starting to change as never before and all eyes were on Texas and the WCCW. We sold out arenas all over the world and not one fan ever left the building until that night's main event was over. Those matches marked the beginning of a new era in professional wrestling that is still going strong today.

Dory Sr.'s oldest son, Dory Jr., was a great athlete and wrestler like his old man. He was what some people called a "scientific" or "pure" wrestler. He and I had a few good matches ourselves and Dory Jr. took home a couple of world titles before he retired.

I always thought the youngest son, Terry, was most like his dad—mean as hell and tough as nails. I had the opportunity to see some of Terry's matches on satellite television in the early nineties when he was wrestling for the ECW (Extreme Championship Wrestling); I enjoyed watching Terry perform. I also tuned in to see him win the ECW World Championship title, which was some match.

Watching Terry that night brought me back to the old days when Dory and I were packing them in the arenas.

Wrestling sure has changed over the years. I was very impressed with the ECW; these guys hit each other with everything in the house and stored stuff under the ring they could pull out and use on one another. Terry won that night, but he sure took some bad bumps. Just as I said before, he was so much like his old man—mean as hell and tough as nails.

Some of the wrestlers from up north who I had done battle with on many occasions would later show up in the Dallas Fort Worth area. As WCCW grew even larger, I would later be elected president of the National Wrestling Alliance and hold that position for many years afterward.

Wrestling had started booming in the late sixties in Texas and we were able to bring in some big boys from up north. One name that sticks in my mind of course is Johnny "The Hammer" Valentine. He and I loved to beat on each other. I do not even remember who won most of our matches. We would just show up in some town and beat each other senseless, sometimes on a nightly basis. Johnny's nickname was "The Hammer" because he had an elbow drop that could hurt you bad if used at the proper time, and he did know what time to use it. Johnny's son, Greg "The Hammer" Valentine would later continue in his father's footsteps. That boy's wrestling style was just like his dad's. Hell, he even looked like his dad, and could also use that elbow just like his old man.

In the seventies, most of all of the big-name wrestlers flew their own planes, or flew with other wrestlers. I had my pilot's license and flew a twin-engine Cessna. One night, Johnny Valentine, Ric Flair, Tim Woods, David Crockett, Bobby Bruggers, and the pilot whose name I cannot recall at this time were in a small, twin-engine airplane when they ran out of fuel on final approach to the New Hanover Airport in Wilmington, North Carolina. Rumor has it that Johnny Valentine—who was sitting up front in the co-pilot's seat—turned around, laughed, and told the other wrestlers in the rear of the plane, "I have some bad news, guys; we just ran out of fuel."

The plane hit the ground and slid on its belly a good one hundred yards until it slammed into an embankment. The plane hit with such force that the pilot's seatbelt broke and he flew through the windshield of the plane and was in a coma for a few weeks before passing away. Johnny Valentine had braced his arms against the dashboard of the plane on impact. When the plane hit, all the rear seats broke loose and the wrestlers in the rear of the plane—along with the seats and baggage—came crashing forward into Johnny, breaking his back in three places. That put an end to his wrestling career and landed him in a wheelchair for the rest of his life. I think he still lives over near Fort Worth somewhere.

Ric Flair, who was around twenty-four at the time of the plane crash, was just starting out in wrestling. He broke his back in one place also, but he was young and healed after a few months, going on to become a legend in the business. The other wrestlers got out with just bruises and scratches, but we lost one of the great wrestlers when Johnny Valentine was forced to retire.

People still ask me all the time if wrestling is fake. How can they ask that question when they see old wrestlers like me? Just look at me. I am sixty-seven years old and I cannot hear a thing without my hearing aids. I can hardly stand without the use of a crutch, much less walk. I have had so many injuries and operations of one kind or another that arthritis has set into almost every joint in my body. I always answer that question by asking them what their definition of fake is.

What many people do not understand is that wrestlers put their asses on the line night after night by doing all those high-risk maneuvers to please the crowds. Oh, there were a lot of times back in the old days of wrestling when some promoter would tell two wrestlers to make the match last longer, maybe show the fans a few fancy moves before a pin. After all, most real fights usually do not last more than a couple of minutes; I think that most fight fans have seen this on the (UFC) Ultimate Fighting Championship. So we would make sure there was some show at the beginning of the match so the fans would get their money's worth. We would intimidate each other and the crowds or show off our muscles. (In my case, it was the Iron Claw.) However, whoever won the match did so by being better, meaner, smarter, and faster than his opponent.

Let's face it, wrestling crowds like to see wrestlers get mad at each other and they like to see blood. If they do not see blood, they think the matches are fake. Fans also like to label everything as good and bad, or good versus evil. It makes for better viewing and understanding. Therefore, if you give your wrestling stars personalities and just let those different personalities develop and clash on their own, it makes for a better show. The fans are all going to tune in next week or go down to the local arena to see the outcome of the feud the two of them started. At WCCW, we would set our shows up like a soap opera on TV. The fans could see the feuds begin, continue, and grow each week in a more or less natural way. What I mean by this is that if both wrestlers get into their good or bad routine, the crowds will usually take over from there and will naturally label one as the hero and one as the villain. The winner would and should always be the better man. I always felt like the outcome of the feud would take care of itself.

All the injuries that wrestlers suffer are real. There are times when wrestlers get carried away or really get mad at their opponent and someone gets hurt. The terrible part is that if they are injured and cannot wrestle the next show, they do not get paid. If they are out of the ring for too long trying to recover from an injury, the promoters may not want them back because the fans will have forgotten them. If wrestling was just about winning or injuring your opponent, then you would only see wrestlers in matches every couple of months or once a year as in boxing and other full-contact sports. The rest of the time that wrestler would be training or recovering from injuries done in his last match. Wrestling is entertainment. These guys have to be in the next town to wrestle the next night or weekend. When a wrestler starts in this business, the pay is so bad that you can hardly cover your expenses. It takes years of matches for a wrestler to get enough experience to be in a main event and make decent money. So there is like a mutual agreement between the two wrestlers—you do not try to hurt me and I will not try to hurt you. No insurance company that I know of will even talk to a wrestler about health insurance, so if the promoter does not carry health insurance, that wrestler is on his own.

Some of the moves I see now on television I would never have attempted back in my day just to please the crowds because I would have been in bed healing instead of in the ring making money. My oldest son, Kevin, use to scare me half to death with some of the things he would do. I have seen that boy jump off the top rope so high he would almost knock the lights above the ring down; I was always worried that someday he was going to break his damn neck. Let us not leave out the fact that the competition in the wrestling business is much fiercer today than in my day. Every wrestler that steps in the ring does so for the recognition, not the money. If you are good and you put on a good match and get yourself recognized and the fans want to see you, the money will just be there.

Other great wrestlers of the good old days that come to mind are Stan Hansen, Bruno Sanmartino, Blackjack Mulligan, and Crusher Stan Stasiak, the "Master of the Heart Punch." Stasiak once sent me to the hospital with that heart punch. He hit me so hard in the chest during a match at the Sportatorium that Doris and the boys took me to Baylor hospital after the match because they thought I was having a heart attack. I was reading something the other day in all that stuff you had printed out for me to read that said I faked that heart attack to bring in a bigger crowd. Let me tell you right now that I do not think that I have ever been hit that hard in my life. I went to the hospital that night because I thought Stasiak had broken my ribcage, not because I thought I was having a heart attack. I did not want Stan Stasiak in Dallas to begin with. We both started wrestling up north as bad guys, or "heels" as they sometimes called us in the business. Our personalities just naturally clashed. He hated me and I hated him. We were both fighting for that recognition and those championship belts back in those days. It made from great matches between the two of us, not to mention more money. We battled for years until one night in a Texas Death Match at Texas Stadium, I put the Abdominal Claw on him and kept it in one place for so long that I wound up doing internal damage to his lower intestines. He had to be carried out of the ring on a stretcher that night and was in the hospital for almost a week before getting out and leaving Texas, never to return to Dallas.

I have been in the ring with so many great wrestlers that it would take days to tell you every name, even if I could remember them all. Any wrestler who lasted more than a few years had to be good or he would not have stayed in the business that long. Professional wrestling will take its toll on your body in just a few short years, so you can imagine what it does to you after twenty or more years of doing battle on sometimes a nightly basis. In my thirty-five-plus-year wrestling career, I have had more than six thousand matches. I won seventy-one percent, with eight percent of my losses coming from disqualifications.

Another question that many fans asked me is about Playboy Gary Hart, a very high-profile manager who handled some of the greatest names in the business. Did we really hate each other, as it seemed on television? The answer to that question would have to be, yes! For those of you who might not know, Gary Hart started out wrestling up north just as I had.

Of course he was never that great of a wrestler and was well known in the business for being a dirty wrestler, always bringing some foreign object into the ring or having one of his friends interfere in his matches. We did not like each other then and we do not like each other now. Gary was injured in the ring up north and gave up wrestling to become a manager. Although I did not like him as a wrestler or a manager, I have to say he managed many wrestlers who went on to become major stars. He was a pain in my ass for many years. One time at the Sportatorium after I had retired, Kerry was getting ready for a shot at the NWA world belt when Gary Hart put up a five thousand-dollar bounty for any wrestler who could injure Kerry and keep him out of the upcoming title match. This caused a lot of problems between the two of us. I will give him credit for being a good manager. Gary Hart did bring good wrestling talent to Dallas where they took on me and my sons for many years. So without the likes of Playboy Gary Hart, the Von Erich family would not have had as many great matches as we did.

The following are the many titles that Fritz Von Erich won in his thirty-five-year career:

WORLD TAG-TEAM TITLE

NATIONAL WRESTLING ALLIANCE (MINNEAPOLIS VERSION)
01/1957—08/1960

AMERICAN WRESTLING ASSOCIATION

08/1960—1991
Ivan Kalmikoff & Karol Kalmikoff
01/08/1957—Defeats Fritz Von Erich & Karl Von Schober in tournament final
Fritz Von Erich & Hans Herman
07/01/1958—Defeats Ivan Kalmikoff & Karol Kalmikoff

NWA UNITED STATES HEAVYWEIGHT TITLE

(CHICAGO & DETROIT VERSION) Fritz Von Erich Defeats Dick the Bruiser
12/01/1961 in Detroit, Michigan
Fritz Von Erich Defeats Lord Athol Layton
08/06/1963 in Detroit, Michigan
Fritz Von Erich Defeats Johnny Valentine
10/19/1963 in Detroit, Michigan

NATIONAL WRESTLING ALLIANCE

07/1948—06/14/1956

AMERICAN WRESTLING ASSOCIATION - OMAHA

06/14/1956–09/07/1963

WORLD HEAVYWEIGHT TITLE

Fritz Von Erich Defeats Vern Gagna, Wins AWA World title
07/31/1962 in Omaha, Nebraska
Fritz Von Erich Defeats Vern Gagna
Fritz Von Erich, wins both AWA and NWA World titles
07/27/1963 in Omaha, Nebraska

TEXAS HEAVYWEIGHT TITLE

Fritz Von Erich
01/05/1965
04/30/1965
01/16/1967

NWA TEXAS HEAVYWEIGHT TAG-TEAM TITLE

Fritz Von Erich & Killer Karl Kox win 06/29/1965 in Houston, Texas
Fritz Von Erich & Duke Keomuka win 03/01/1966 in Dallas, Texas

NWA AMERICAN HEAVYWEIGHT TITLE

Fritz Von Erich wins titles in:
06/06/1966
08/04/1966
03/27/1967
06/03/1968
08/04/1969
06/14/1970
02/22/1971
08/07/1973
04/18/1974
12/29/1974
04/12/1977
12/12/1977
Retirement Match—06/14/1982

NWA AMERICAN HEAVYWEIGHT TAG-TEAM TITLE

Fritz Von Erich wins
02/21/1967—with Waldo Von Erich
1968—with Billy Red Lyons
07/19/1968—with Grizzly Smith
1969—with Dan Miller
03/21/1969—with Fred Curry
01/25/1972—with Dean Ho

NWA WORLD INTERNATIONAL HEAVYWEIGHT TITLE

Fritz Von Erich defeats the Giant Baba in Japan
12/03/1966

NWA INTERNATIONAL TAG-TEAM TITLE
Fritz Von Erich wins
04/18/1973—with Killer Karl Krupp

TEXAS BRASS KNUCKS TITLE
04/15/1958—Fritz Von Erich

WCCW WORLD SIX-MAN TAG-TEAM TITLE
05/06/1984

The very first wrestling picture made of Fritz that he signed himself in the early 1950s, just before the Iron Claw

Kevin, Fritz, and David Von Erich

To Ron -
one of the best friends
the Von Erich family
ever had -
Fritz Von Erich
THE VON ERICHS
David
Fritz
Kerry

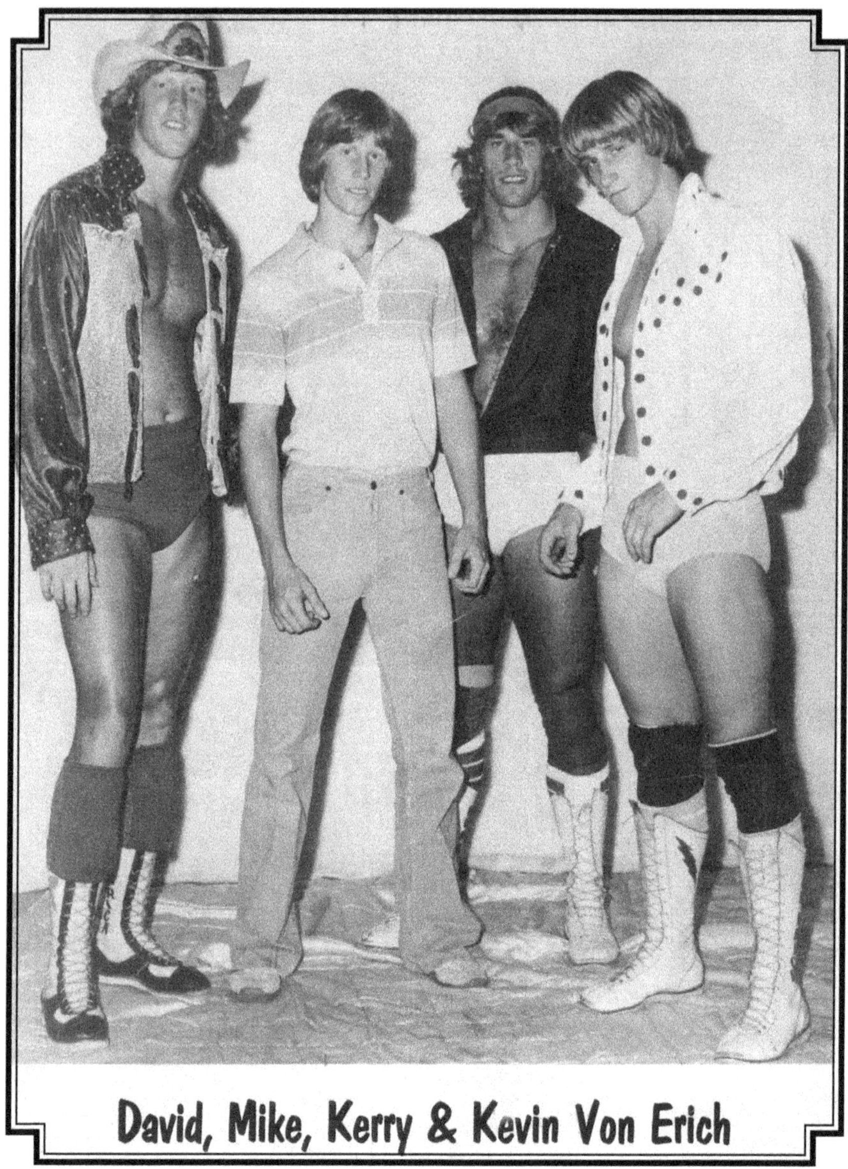

David, Mike, Kerry & Kevin Von Erich

Kevin Von Erich
World Class
CHAMPIONSHIP
WRESTLI

Kerry Von Erich

CHAPTER 8

When David, my second-oldest son, graduated from Lake Dallas High School, he accepted an athletic scholarship to North Texas State University right behind Kevin. David was six feet eight inches tall and played both football and basketball. This was a talent that was something very rare in college sports. Nevertheless, after Kevin entered into the wrestling business, a very short time later David walked into my office, sat down, and said he wanted more than anything to join Kevin and me in the ring. David said he had given the idea of a career a lot of thought and felt he was making the right decision in making professional wrestling his chosen career. I really hated to see David drop out of North Texas State. I tried my best to persuade him to wait another year until he graduated. His grades were very good and he seemed to have so much going for him. He and I talked for a while and I told him that I would have to think about it and it might not hurt for him to give it more thought as well.

Kevin first came into professional wrestling after his knee had healed from a football injury he sustained his senior year at North Texas State. Kevin knew his football career was over and, like his father, he still wanted more than anything to make his living in sports.

David usually followed in Kevin's footsteps, so I was not really surprised that David and I were discussing him dropping out of North Texas State and joining Kevin and me in the ring. David was very excited that day and could not wait to tell me all the plans he and Kevin had made concerning their new careers.

Ever since they were young boys, David had always wanted to be a pro wrestler and Kevin wanted to be a pro football player. When Kevin and David were growing up, David would always pretend he was a wrestler. He would wear his housecoat around the house as if it was his ring jacket and would make everyone call him David Von Erich instead of David Adkisson. Meanwhile, Kevin would talk David into playing football with him and the game seemed to always end in a wrestling match between the two boys. David would tackle Kevin, and instead of getting off him after the play was over, David would get Kevin in a headlock or try to put the Iron Claw on him.

Both boys were in excellent shape when they turned to me for advice and had worked hard over the years building their bodies. I was not worried about them getting hurt while in the ring. Wrestling had changed so much since I had my first match back in the early 1950s. With their old dad running the show, I would be able to keep them close to home, which I knew would be one of their mother's immense concerns.

Kevin and David had been in the wrestling business just over two years. Their careers in wrestling looked very promising and the two of them were in big demand all over the country as a tag team. One day, when I least expected it, Kevin, David, and Kerry walked into my office to inform me of their big plans, which included Kerry dropping out of the University of Houston and joining the other two in the ring. I knew it was bound to happen. Those three always stuck together and one would always follow the other. As it turned out, Kerry had been after Kevin and David for months to ask me what I thought about him dropping out of college and joining his brothers in the ring. I was not surprised when the three of them came into my office that day to tell me of their big plans. Both Kevin and David were excited about the three of them being together in the ring, so they made it very hard for me to say no.

David was a very smart young man. Besides being a very good wrestler and all-around athlete, he had a good head on his shoulders for business and could talk his way into or out of just about anything. David was also showing a big interest in what went on in the front office. He would sit with me for hours listening in on my meetings and trying to get a feel for the business while Kevin and Kerry were wondering whose house the next party would be held at. David was always coming up with new ideas that would later lead to sold-out matches at Texas Stadium and other venues around the country. I always thought David could have gone really far in the world of wrestling, both as a wrestler and as a promoter. He was a real natural. The idea the three of them had come to me with that morning had been mostly David's doing. It involved the three of them and the beginning of a six-man tag team event and the new WCCW Six-Man World Championship title.

Just as my boys were getting started with their wrestling careers, I was starting to wind down. All those years of wrestling and all the injuries I had sustained in my 35-plus-year career were starting to catch up with me. I made up my mind that it was time to say farewell to all my wonderful fans out there in the wrestling world and focus my attention on promoting. In the summer of 1982, I announced that my last match would be against 450-pound King Kong Bundy, who then held the American heavyweight championship belt, a title that I had held longer than anyone in the wrestling business.

Bundy had been the American heavyweight champion for only a few months and I wanted to take that heavyweight title away from him before I said farewell. When he and I stepped into that ring in front of 30,000 screaming fans in Texas Stadium, I was as pumped up for a match as I had ever been in my life. There was no way this guy was going to beat me in front of all my hometown fans and keep the belt that had been mine for so many years.

The rules of the match were that falls could take place and count either in the ring or on the field of Texas Stadium. I started the match by throwing Bundy out of the ring, and that would be where most of the wrestling took place. He and I wrestled in the ring, out of the ring, and even in the crowd.

Eventually, Bundy grabbed hold of a chair and hit me in the back of the head. He knocked me down to the Astroturf outside the ring and started pounding on me. When I finally got out from under him and back on my feet, I grabbed the metal chair myself from ringside and hit him over the head. Then I dropped the chair and applied the Iron Claw to the top of the head of King Kong Bundy. I had Bundy busted open in no time flat. At that moment, at Texas Stadium with the crowd screaming their heads off, I think I put more into that hold than I ever had in the past. Bundy was screaming for me to let him go; he told the referee that he'd had enough as blood ran down the side of his face. The next thing I knew, the referee was raising my hand and giving me the American heavyweight belt that I had held for so long in my career. That was a night I will remember for the rest of my life. As I said goodbye to pro wrestling, Doris and all five of the boys were at my side, and three of my sons were dressed in their wrestling tights awaiting their upcoming match with the Freebirds.

The end of my career was not a sad thing because I was more or less turning the business over to my three oldest sons. I was the proudest father on Earth with nothing left to prove to the wrestling world. With wrestling behind me, Doris and I made the decision to build our dream home in East Texas. I was going to sit back and relax—spend the rest of my life hunting and fishing with a little promoting on the side. After months of looking at land all over East Texas, we finally found the perfect spot to build our dream house near Edom, Texas.

Kevin, David, and Kerry were wrestling to sold-out stadiums all over the world. The three of them were changing wrestling history as I had never seen it change during the course of my career. They were catching the interest of the younger crowds and had won the Six-Man World Tag-Team Championship title against another great young tag-team, the Fabulous Freebirds from Atlanta, Georgia. As soon as the championship match ended that night, those three boys were on top of the world. Wrestlers from around the world were trying to find good tag-team partners to put together a three-man team to take on the Von Erich boys; all of a sudden, the six-man title was starting to get a lot of attention and promoters were trying to find larger arenas to hold the new younger crowds.

David was to be touring Japan for about three weeks; upon his return to Dallas, he was booked to wrestle Ric Flair for the NWA World Heavyweight title. David had been in the business over five years and his career was going great. He was telling everyone he would be the next NWA world heavyweight champion and I believed he could do it.

Early on the morning of February 9, 1984, I received an overseas call that awoke me from my sleep. A voice on the other end of the line was telling me that my son, David, had been found dead in his hotel room in Japan. He was twenty-five years old.

It was a few hours before Doris and I could find out all the details. Before going to Japan, David had caught what he thought was a stomach virus. Before he left the United States he told a trainer that he was sick to his stomach but thought he would be all right. When he got to Japan, he went straight to his hotel room and stayed in his bed until it was time to wrestle that night. He wrestled even though he had a slight fever and was still sick to his stomach. It had been a long match, lasting almost to the time limit with David taking some bad bumps.

That night, David had taken a very hard hit to the lower stomach area that caused his intestine to rupture. He was not aware of the seriousness of what had happen to him. After the match, a couple of other wrestlers tried to get him to see a doctor, but he told everyone that he was going to be all right—that it was just a bad stomach virus. What David did not know was that the blow to the stomach had made his condition much worse. David insisted, saying that he just needed to go to his hotel room and get some sleep, and that if he started feeling any worse, he would call the team doctor.

The next morning, one of the trainers had tried to telephone David because he had missed an early morning appointment. When David did not pick up the phone, the trainer and one of the referees went to his room to check on him. David would not answer the door, so after several loud knocks, the hotel manager and security were called. All four men entered David's room, where they found David laying face down on the floor beside his bed. It appeared that David had gotten out of bed sometime during the night and tried to make it to the bathroom, where he fell to the floor and died of heart failure.

I felt the terrible pain of losing a son start building up inside me. I was a very devoted Christian at the time of David's death—just as I had promised the Lord years earlier—but I was again starting to ask myself questions just as I had done after Jack Jr. had passed away. How could the Lord take yet another one of my sons when he was still so young?

After the funeral, Kevin and Kerry, who were both rated among the top ten wrestlers in the world by *Ringside Magazine*, were both given the opportunity to step in for their brother David and face Ric Flair for the NWA heavyweight title. Both Kevin and Kerry were so evenly matched that the two brothers decided to flip a coin in the middle of the ring on Friday night to a sold-out crowd at the Sportatorium, and Kerry won the toss.

On May 6, 1984, in front of 50,000 emotional fans at Texas Stadium, the largest wrestling crowd to ever assemble for a match screamed for Kerry, who came to the ring wearing a light-colored ring jacket with yellow rose embroidery on the back that said "In Memory of David." He climbed into the ring after handing out yellow roses just as his brother had done so many times in the past. In front of the largest wrestling crowd ever in Texas Stadium history, Kerry won the NWA World Heavyweight Championship title for his brother David and got the three-count on Ric Flair in the middle of the ring with a sunset flip.

The crowd went wild after Kerry won that match. I was very proud of what Kerry had done for his brother David, but I still felt that something had again been ripped from my body. Doris, the boys, and I had all turned to the Lord for some relief from the pain we felt.

We would tell one another that the Lord had his reason for taking David away from us so early in his life. It was not for us to question the Lord's decision. But in the back of my mind was a question that I would keep asking myself over and over again. Why, oh why, had the Lord seen fit to take two of my sons from me? Not only could I not get David off my mind, but thoughts of Jack Jr. came rushing back to me stronger than ever before, leaving me numb inside.

******

News articles were taken from the Dallas Times Herald: All articles are printed as they appeared.

DAVID VON ERICH DIES—

Wrestler suffers apparent heart failure in Tokyo

By: Mark Edgar
Staff Writer of the *News*, February 16, 1984

David Von Erich, 25-year-old member of a well-known local wrestling family respected for their fair play and showmanship, died Friday of apparent heart failure in his hotel room after a match in Tokyo, Japan, family members said.

Von Erich, whose real name was David Adkisson, recently suffered a concussion at a match in Dallas. Nevertheless, relatives said, he appeared to be in top physical condition before he left Tuesday for the three-week overseas tour.

"This was a case of overexertion," said his brother, Kevin. "He was in good condition, but he tended to push himself too far. Sometimes he would be so tired he would even throw up. He never rested enough.

"A lot of wrestlers get a second wind. David used to get a second, third and fourth wind. This time he just didn't get back up."

Von Erich comes from the popular wrestling family— featuring Fritz Von Erich and his sons, Kevin, 26, Kerry, 23, Michael, 19, and Chris, 13.

Kevin and Kerry canceled a scheduled match Friday at the Dallas Sportatorium after learning of their brother's death.

Von Erich was found dead on the floor of his Takariawa Tobu Hotel room by a referee after he failed to show in the hotel lobby to leave for another match, said the hotel manager, Hiroaki Tak-ido.

Results of an autopsy were not available late Friday. An inquest is scheduled Saturday, Tokyo authorities said.

Authorities who made a preliminary examination of the body said the cause of death was heart failure, said Fritz Von Erich, whose real name is Jack Adkisson.

Kevin said a referee in Tokyo told him his brother had complained about being sick during a limousine ride to the hotel after a match a few hours before he died. He went to his room and refused offers to go out for dinner, saying he wanted to go to bed, Kevin said.

"He was a cowboy. He liked to take one or two drinks after a match. He was in no way, shape or form involved in drugs," Kevin said. During an interview at his Lake Dallas home Friday, Fritz Von Erich said, "He was a great kid. I love all my boys but he was something special. We'll all eventually be in heaven."

Billed as the Iron Nail, David Von Erich was scheduled to fight a champion Japanese wrestler Feb. 23.

Ringside magazine, a major wrestling publication, called David Von Erich "one of the top five wrestlers in the world" in its September issue. "He has nowhere to go but up," the magazine said.

Ed Watt, who arranges matches at the Sportatorium, said Von Erich "had the potential to become the next Heavyweight Champion." With his brothers—and under the tutelage of his now-retired father—David was considered one of the kings of the mat. In a profession long associated with theatrics, the Von Eriches' clean-cut, straightforward image stood out.

Their critics denounced them as "pretty boys" who catapulted to fame on their father's mostly bad-guy image and managerial skills.

Before local contests, mostly teen-age girls with offerings of cakes, embroidered shirts, photos, and rings swarmed the Von Erich brothers.

Family members said they get 800 fans letters weekly. Von Erich was a prominent high school athlete at Lake Dallas High School and went to North Texas State University, where he played basketball and football before leaving early to wrestle professionally. He had been groomed as a child for the job.

His father set up a ring at the family's Lake Dallas home, teaching each son to wrestle at about age 6.

In an interview with the *Dallas Morning News* last May, David said, "I'd catch a touchdown pass in high school and the coach would go crazy and the fans would go crazy. Nevertheless, it did not mean anything to me unless I saw my dad in the stands clapping. ...If we were not hustling, we would hear from him. It would be like a bolt of lightning."

David was known as a close-in body fighter, able to apply arm and leg locks so tightly they stopped the flow of blood— almost like his father's once-deadly Iron Claw trademark.

In addition to his father and brothers, he is survived by his wife, Tricia, and mother, Doris Adkisson. The couple had no children.

FANS PAY RESPECTS TO DAVID VON ERICH

Staff writer Stephen G. Bloom and Shelley Smith, in Tokyo, contributed to this report.

Dallas Times Herald

Two fans of champion wrestler David Adkisson Von Erich walk away following memorial services Wednesday at the First Baptist Church in Denton. A Lake Dallas resident, David Von Erich was found dead in his Tokyo Hotel room.

His death was attributed to an intestinal disease. The 25- year-old man's funeral attracted major media coverage and approximately 3,500 persons attended, including a contingent of Lewisville area fans.

"They wanted me to work today," she said—a true die-hard wrestling fan. "I told them, 'No way.' Maybe tonight, but not today.'"

About noon, the cortege pulled in the gates of the cemetery. Police gently held the crowd back from the Von Erich family.

"David is with the Lord Jesus," Rev McCombs said. "Watch over him, Lord, as he's learning the ropes up there in heaven."

Afterward, wrestler Chris (The Gentleman) Adams walked from the casket, dodging the outstretched hands of fans. Duke Keomuka, who retired from wrestling 12 years ago, wiped away a tear with a gnarled finger.

Nine-year-old Michael Gilson, wearing a cowboy hat, took the arrangement of artificial flowers from his mother, Paulette, and walked it shyly under the tent, to place it among the rest of the yellow roses.

As the child retreated, Sondra Adkisson, David Von Erich's cousin, watched him and said, "Thank you, son, you're very sweet." Then she explained, "Fritz said the crowd is what made them, and he wanted the crowd to be a part of this. It's a lot harder on the family this way, but the crowd loved the boys."

Despite exhortations from police, the crowd refused to disperse after the service. They milled around the casket as it was lowered into the ground.

Then as the hundreds of flower arrangements from the church were laid at graveside, most of the hundreds of sprays of roses, carnations, daisies and the yellow roses—David's favorite flower.

One arrangement was in the shape of Texas; another featured a pair of leather cowboy boots and a floral cross.

Among the wrestling world's four luminaries present were Ric Flair, Gene Kiniski, Dory and Terry Funk, Verne Gagne, Duke: Keomuka, Brian Adias, Iceman, King Parsons, Chris Adams, the Super Ds and Jose Lothario. I tried to avoid the crush of the fans; the tribe of wrestlers was ushered through a side entrance and shown to reserved seats at the front. They were hulking men many with scarred faces and broken noses. Known for their theatrics in the ring, they were quiet and solemn. Although a rival of the Von Erich's, Ric Flair was there to share in the family's grief.

"The fact that we were enemies in the ring didn't have anything to do with the tremendous amount of respect I had for him," said Flair, who beat David for a national championship last year.

Absent, though, were the Freebirds, a three-man wrestling team, and avowed archenemies of the Von Erich brothers. "They have enough respect for the fans not to attend," referee David Manning said. "But they told me they will miss David."

Also absent were television camera crews. Earlier plans to film the service for a later telecast were dropped when Fritz Von Erich banned cameras from the church.

Sunshine, former valet to wrestling villain Gorgeous Jimmy Garvin, arrived just before the service began. Her mascara and purple eye shadows were smeared from tears. "I didn't believe the news when I first heard it," said Sunshine, who last year was spanked at ringside by David Von Erich. "David befriended me and I will miss him. It's going to be hard on everyone."

During the service, sobs from the fans drifted down from the choir loft. Young girls held each other's hands for support. "David did more living in 25 years than most people do in 70 years," said Rev. L.L. Armstrong, one of three ministers who delivered eulogies.

WITH DAVID VON ERICH GONE—
'Rasslin ain't gonna be the same'

Dallas Times Herald
Thursday, February 16, 1984:

"David was gorgeous—fire and ice," said Justa Soehig of Arlington. "You could feel the electricity when he stepped into the ring."

That electricity obviously touched more than wet-eyed adolescents. The funeral drew the elderly along with the young professionals, truck drivers, welders, waiters, and Japanese journalism. There were workers who had been laid off and others who missed work.

In addition, there were wrestlers, scores of hulking men with pummeled features.

There was Ric Flair, with his bleached-blond hair flowing to the collar of his grey pinstripe suit. The near great and former great from the ring pined for him: Gene Kiniski, Terry Funk, Funk Jr., Gentleman Chris Adams, Jose Lathario, Johnny Mantel, Iceman King Parsons, and Brian Adias.

Aside from an occasional cry of, "Look over there, isn't that somebody?" the spectators were restrained and solemn as they filled the sanctuary. They dabbed their eyes with shredded tissues and quietly shared their feelings for Von Erich and the Sportatorium on South Industrial Boulevard, where he performed. The mix was broken only once by a small boy who, at the request of another youngster, demonstrated Von Erich's famous "Iron Claw" grip on his unsuspecting bystander.

The organist played traditional hymns, then Beethoven's Fur Elise as the Von Erich wrestling dynasty walked in. They came as the Adkisson family, their real name, and a simple, tight-knit local clan: Father Jack (alias Fritz), mother Doris, brothers Kevin, Kerry, Michael and Chris, and David's wife, Tricia; and cousins, uncles, aunts and grandparents, one by one, three Baptist ministers inched through the yellow-rose bouquets around.

Von Erich's closed coffin was carried to the pulpit, where family members had placed two color portraits of the wrestler wearing his cowboy hat.

The first minister quietly told the congregation of Von Erich's "match with the devil" and how he was victorious because he had reached out to Christ, as had his brothers on the tag team.

The second minister used a more fiery yea-I-say-unto- you approach that drew sporadic "That's right's" and a few "Ameen's!" The crowd was with him; it knew Von Erich had been born again. It wanted to hear how it could meet him again someday.

The third minister squelched the mood, though, with solemn talk of death.

As the final prayer was said, many mourners began to weep. The emotion swelled as the family filed out. The balcony resembled a Beatles-era scene, with hundreds of sobbing young girls clutching tissues to their faces. As the family members passed, people gently reached out to touch and say, "God bless you."

The family, flanked by bodyguards in black cowboy hats, quickly climbed into the train of white limousines. However, as hundreds pressed toward him, Fritz Von Erich stepped out of the car, shook a few hands, accepted sympathy cards pushed out to him and hugged the few who broke past the bodyguards.

He climbed back into the car and led the procession from north I-35 to Grove Hill Cemetery in Dallas, where hundreds more people were waiting.

Thousands crushed together around grave markers of the lesser known, straining to hear the brief graveside service. As the family took a few last minutes alone with David Von Erich's casket, the fans formed a path to the cars, their last chance to see their heroin congregated.

"We're just overwhelmed," Fritz Von Erich told the fans after the funeral. "We love all of you."

As the family's limousine drove away, Ron Cook, a truck driver from Dallas, slowly shook his head and said what so many seemed to be thinking: "Rasslin ain't never gonna be the same again!"

WRESTLING CARD PAYS TRIBUTE TO DAVID VON ERICH

By: Stan Hovatter Jr.
Published, May 3, 1986 the *Dallas Morning News*

In three years, the "Parade of Champions: A Memorial to David Von Erich" has developed into one of the nation's top professional wrestling events, but to the Von Erich family, it is more than huge crowds and championship matches.

"It's not just a great card with great wrestlers," said Kevin Von Erich, eldest of the wrestling brothers. "It's like a reunion of people who loved my brother David."The World Class Wrestling Association has put together another main-event card in memory of David Von Erich, who died at age 25 of enteritis, an inflammation of the intestinal tract. At the time of his death, David was the No. 1- ranked contender for the World Championship title.

The third Parade of Champions, beginning at 3 p.m. at Texas

Stadium, features two world championship matches and two special events, a Barbed Wire match and a Pigsty Mud Match.

Wrestling in two of the main events will be veteran Bruiser Brody. He will take on WCWA world champion Rick Rood in one and then try to settle a long-standing feud with Terry Gordy, one of the Fabulous Freebirds, in the Barbed Wire Match.

The Freebirds—Gordy, Michael Hayes and Buddy Roberts—put their world six-man tag-team titles on the line against Kevin, Kerry and Lance Von Erich in the other world championship match. Kevin and Kerry are two of David's brothers and Lance is a cousin.

Fritz Von Erich, patriarch of the famous wrestling family, will be at ringside for the lumberjack-style, elimination tag-team match, in which 14 men bearing straps surround the ring and chase back in any wrestler who might stray outside. As participants are pinned, they are eliminated from the match.

"It (the Parade of Champions) is a very personal thing with us," said Fritz, who retired as an active wrestler in 1982 at age 51. "There is always a special motivation for us at this event."

The first Parade of Champions, in May 1984, drew more than 41,000 fans, the largest in-person attendance for a professional wrestling card ever. That was the year Fritz came out of retirement to help sons Kevin and Mike win the world six-man title. Last year, more than 33,000 turned out for the second Parade of Champions, also held at Texas Stadium.

For the third consecutive year, proceeds from the event will go to charity. Beneficiaries the first two years were Temple Christian Academy and the Crippled Children's Home of Dallas.

"We feel like David's image was tied in with children," said Fritz.

"David loved anything that had to do with children. We haven't decided yet where the proceeds from this year's event will go, but I am sure that it will have something to do with kids."

******

The following are some of the titles that David Von Erich won in his short career:

NWA WORLD TAG-TEAM TITLES

Kevin and David Von Erich—April 7, 1978
Dallas, Texas
Kevin and David Von Erich—February 1981
Houston, Texas

WCCW WORLD SIX-MAN TAG-TEAM TITLE

Kevin, David, and Kerry—July 4, 1983
Fort Worth, Texas
Kevin, David, and Kerry—December 2, 1983
Dallas, Texas

TEXAS HEAVYWEIGHT TITLE

David Von Erich—September 10, 1978
Dallas, Texas
David Von Erich—February 16, 1979
Dallas, Texas
David Von Erich—August 6, 1980
Dallas, Texas

TEXAS HEAVYWEIGHT TAG-TEAM TITLE

Kevin and David Von Erich–April 7, 1978
Houston, Texas
Kevin and David Von Erich–September 4, 1978
Fort Worth, Texas

CHAPTER 9

After David's death, myself and the rest of the family turned to the Lord to help us try to understand why this had to happen, especially at such a big time in David's life. Kevin and Kerry really took his death hard. They were talking about how they would have to vacate the world six-man tag team belts when Mike stepped up and announced that he would like to take David's place.

Mike had always been a great athlete but he was plagued by one injury after another throughout his high school sports career. Despite that, he worked out hard every day and the only thing on his mind was to follow in his brothers' wrestling footsteps, trying to be just as good as his brother David was. I was not sure what to say about Mike's decision to take David's place. Mike had never really indicated to me that he wanted to become a wrestler until after David's death. I was very worried about Mike's shoulder and all the injuries he had suffered in high school athletics, plus the fact that he was only eighteen years old and really should have been trying to get into a good college. Mike said he had not yet made up his mind about college and a career, so I reluctantly agreed to let Mike wrestle after both Kevin and Kerry said that they would watch after him and not let anything happen to him. Kevin and Kerry started training Mike the very next day, showing him all the tricks of the trade and preparing him to enter the ring as a professional wrestler and fill his brother David's shoes.

Mike started his professional wrestling career in November 1984. In his first match at Reunion Arena in Dallas, Mike defeated Skandar Akbar before a packed house and was already on his way to stardom. He then won the six-man world title with Kevin and Kerry and later, when Kerry was on the same card to wrestle Ric Flair for the world heavyweight title, I came out of retirement to tag with Kevin and Mike at a packed Texas Stadium for the Parade Of Champions against the Fabulous Freebirds. That was another moment in my life that I will never forget.

Mike's career was soaring. In fact, everyone was saying he was the best athlete in the Von Erich family. On August 4, 1985, Mike won the NWA American Heavyweight title and was doing great, except for the bad shoulder that had bothered him since high school. After watching Mike for months and noticing that he was still having problems with that shoulder, I insisted he take some time off and have a surgeon take a look at it. We took Mike to one of the best sports surgeons in the Dallas Fort Worth area, who assured us that the shoulder would improve with surgery.

After several visits and routine tests, we scheduled the shoulder surgery, which was described by the doctor as a fairly standard shoulder operation. Mike should recover with no problems and be back to wrestling within a few months, we were told.

The surgery lasted a couple of hours and Mike was recovering nicely when he suddenly took a turn for the worse and was placed in critical condition. The doctor discovered that toxic shock syndrome had attacked Mike's body. Toxic shock is a deadly virus that in most cases is fatal. Mike's kidneys collapsed, most of his major organs shut down, and his body temperature rose to a near-fatal 107 degrees, staying there for hours before the staff at the hospital could get it to stabilize.

Nobody could explain to us what had happened to Mike in such a short time. The doctor who had performed the surgery told us he had turned Mike over to a specialist who was with Mike at that very moment and would come down to talk with us as soon as he knew something.

Later, Dr. Bill Sutker, the infectious disease specialist who was taking over Mike's case, came into the waiting room and told me that Mike had practically no chance of living longer than another thirty minutes to an hour. So many major organs had shut down in Mike's body that he did not think Mike could hold on much longer. Dr. Sutker also told us that it was very rare for a male to be infected with toxic shock syndrome, and that of all the males who had contracted the disease throughout the county, almost all had contracted it after surgery, and all had died after hours of high fever and the failure of one major organ after another. Dr. Sutker said that he did not want to lie to us, but that so very little was known about the disease that he and his staff did not know how to treat Mike. All that was possible was being done to find a treatment Mike would respond to, and Dr. Sutker had been on the phone with the head of the Center for Disease Control gathering all the information he could on this somewhat rare disease.

After everyone in the waiting room was told what the doctor had said, our family and about twenty-five of our close friends all got on our knees and started to pray for Mike while the doctors continued to help him battle for his life. Repeatedly I prayed to the Lord, "Please do not take Mike away from us, too." About two hours later, as we were all getting up off our knees,

Doctor Sutker came back into the waiting room and announced that he could not explain it medically but that Mike had taken a slight turn for the better and was showing signs of improvement. "We were successful in getting his fever down to around 103 degrees, where Mike has started responding to treatment," the doctor said. Everyone in the room was speechless.

Kevin organized a press conference that morning and thanked all the Von Erich fans for their support and prayers. "A miracle took place last night," Kevin said. The doctors all nodded their heads in agreement. "Without the fans' prayers and support I do not think my little brother Mike would be alive at this moment. All the Von Erich family thanks each and every one of you for your support."

During the next two weeks that Mike was in the hospital, the main switchboard was taking an average of four hundred calls an hour, twenty-four hours a day, from fans all over the world who were pulling for Mike's recovery. Baylor medical officials said they had never seen such a response. There had not even been that many calls when President Kennedy had been rushed to Parkland Hospital in 1963, they said.

Later, Baylor Medical Center President Boone Powell, Jr. announced that so much had been learned about the disease during Mike's illness that Baylor would be opening the Von Erich Infectious Disease Center as a permanent part of Baylor Hospital in Dallas. Dr. Bill Sutker would head it.

In 1985, Mike was voted Most Inspirational Athlete of the Year by the readers of *Pro Wrestling Illustrated*. However, he had to sit out of the athletic world for many months while his body recovered from its near-fatal shock.

Mike eventually did come back to the ring, but in my opinion he never fully recovered from toxic shock, either emotionally or physically. The Mike after toxic shock was different from the Mike of before.

I spent many hours watching Mike during the day as he tried to build his body back into shape at the hospital. He was not as successful as he wanted to be and that upset him to no end. Mike was not handling the situation well at all and would get mad at the nurses trying to help him. The always cheery little brother had undergone a distinct personality change that started to show itself shortly after Mike was well on his way to recovery.

When Doris and I spoke with the doctors about Mike's change, they told us that severe personality changes and emotional difficulties were to be expected. They also warned us that a patient who has had extremely high body temperatures over a long period of time could suffer minor or even major brain damage. Only time would tell.

That night at the hospital, when the doctors told Doris and me that

Mike might not make it, they also warned us there was a chance he could lose both feet and both hands due to the extremely low blood pressure that had lasted for hours.

When the nurse wheeled Mike out the door from Intensive Care, everyone was so relieved that he appeared to be on his way to recovery. However, Doris told me later that she knew deep in her heart that other damage would show up later.

******

News articles taken from the *Dallas Morning News* archives: all articles are printed as they appeared.

MIKE VON ERICH IN CRITICAL CONDITION— Dallas wrestler has toxic shock syndrome

By: Rita Rubin
Published, August 31, 1985

Dallas wrestler Mike Von Erich was hospitalized in critical condition Friday with toxic shock syndrome—a potentially fatal infection rarely found in men.

"Last night was really scary—scary to the point it was almost hopeless," Kevin Von Erich said at a news conference Friday morning at Baylor University Medical Center, where his brother was hospitalized. "Folks, let me tell you, a miracle took place, the miracle is that we have Mike today."

By late Friday evening, the young wrestler's condition seemed somewhat improved. Hospital officials said his temperature had dropped to 101 degrees and, rather than describing his prognosis as guarded, said his condition was critical.

Since the syndrome was first described in medical literature in 1978, 2,815 cases have been reported to the U.S. Centers for Disease Control, said Dr. Lee Harrison, an epidemiologist with the CDC in Atlanta. The vast majority of cases—2,255—were linked to tampon use in menstruating women.

Only 146 men contracted the syndrome, usually just after surgery. The death rate in men is 7.5 percent, nearly twice the 4.2 percent rate in women, Harrison said.

The bacterium that causes toxic shock syndrome apparently entered Mike Von Erich's body through a surgical incision made last week to repair his dislocated left shoulder, said Dr. William Sutker, a Baylor specialist in infectious diseases called in to assist in the case. Kevin Von Erich said his brother injured his shoulder in June when he won a Middle East wrestling title in Israel.

Mike Von Erich, 21, whose real name is Adkisson, was discharged Monday from Morton Cancer and Research Hospital after undergoing surgery a few days earlier. Sutker said Von Erich was one of many non-cancer patients who receive treatment at Morton.

"When he was released from the hospital Monday, he was in very good condition," Sutker said at the Baylor press conference. "It (toxic shock) is only very indirectly related to the operation. The operation was a success, and everything went well as far as the repair to his shoulder."

Jennifer Coleman, Baylor director of public relations, related the chronology of Mike's illness: On Tuesday, Von Erich became confused and feverish. He was readmitted Wednesday to Morton. Sutker was called in to confer with Mike's doctor. The decision was made to transfer him to Baylor, where he arrived at 12:30 p.m. Thursday.

"His training and the fact he was in such good physical shape is probably the only reason he is still alive," Sutker said.

Von Erich's kidney function was "minimal" although he was not yet on dialysis, Sutker said. He is receiving antibiotics, but the main treatment for the toxic shock syndrome is life support to maintain breathing, a regular heartbeat and normal blood pressure, Sutker said.

"There are tubes coming out of everywhere you could imagine," Kevin Von Erich said. "My brother looks terrible to me. His temperature went to almost 107 degrees. He has been sedated, and he has had to have muscle relaxers so he does not fight the tubes in him."

Toxic shock syndrome is caused by Staphylococcus aureus, a common species of bacteria often found on skin and in people's nose and other body cavities. According to a CDC study, about 15 percent of Staphylococcus aureus bacteria produce the poison that causes toxic shock syndrome.

Symptoms of toxic shock syndrome include high fever, low blood pressure, dizziness upon standing, a sunburn-like rash, vomiting, and diarrhea.

Not everyone exposed to the poison-producing bacteria develops toxic shock syndrome, said the CDC's Harrison.

"You have to have the right combination of the right wound, the right bug and factors we may not understand all the coming together and producing the syndrome," Harrison said in a phone interview. Some people exposed to the bacterium might only develop a fever for a few days and recover, Harrison said. Others might have antibodies that defend them against the infection, he said.

MIKE VON ERICH IMPROVES SLIGHTLY— Temperature down; wrestler still listed as critical

By: Annette Bernhard
Published, September 1, 1985

Kevin and Kerry Von Erich called it a miracle and credited the collective prayers of thousands of fans.

Their brother and fellow scion of the well-known wrestling clan, Mike Von Erich, showed signs of improvement Saturday in his battle against toxic shock syndrome, said doctors and family members.

"At 4:00 a.m. my mother asked him if he was feeling any pain and to let her know how he was feeling," said 28-year- old Kevin, fighting back tears at a Saturday news conference at Baylor University Medical Center. "He squeezed her hand."

It was the first time the 21-year-old wrestler, whose real last name is Adkisson, had been able to respond to anyone since he was hospitalized Thursday with a fever that reached 107 degrees, family members said. He remained in critical condition Saturday but his fever was maintained just slightly above normal at 98.8 degrees, doctors said. He contracted toxic shock syndrome shortly after undergoing surgery for a dislocated left shoulder last week.

"His improvement is a miracle and there's no fluke about it," said Kerry Von Erich, age 25.

When doctors told the family Thursday night that they had given up hope, Kerry said, family and friends knelt in prayer. As they finished, he said, doctors returned and told them that his fever had dropped to 101 degrees.

By Saturday afternoon, the young wrestler's fever had dropped to 98.8 degrees, said Dr. William Sutker, a Baylor specialist in infectious diseases called in to assist in the case. Sutker said Mike is not comatose but is very weak and heavily sedated. He cannot speak because he breathes with the aid of a respirator, the doctor said.

"His condition is improving, but we're still not out of the woods yet, as he is still in critical condition," Sutker said. "Any small improvement is encouraging but that does not in any way eliminate any danger."

Sutker said doctors were able to maintain Mike Von Erich's blood pressure Saturday and they began using a dialysis machine to improve his kidney function. Sutker said that if doctors continue to see progress within the next 24 to 48 hours, Mike's condition may be upgraded.

Kevin and Kerry urged fans not to call the hospital but to send letters and cards. Hospital officials said switchboard operators have received as many as 100 calls per hour from fans. Some callers offered their kidneys and other organs to help the popular wrestler, they said.

The family has encountered agony before. Patriarch Fritz Adkisson, known in the ring as Fritz Von Erich, and his wife Doris have seen two of their sons die.

Six-year-old Jack Jr. was electrocuted in 1959 in a freak accident. David, 25, died in February 1984 of acute enteritis in a Tokyo hotel room while on a Japanese wrestling tour.

MIKE VON ERICH WINS BOUT—Toxic shock victim expects to wrestle again

By: Rita Rubin
Published, September 24, 1985

He is nearly 50 pounds thinner, his voice tires easily, and his left arm hangs in a sling, but make no mistake about it: Mike Von Erich has won the match of his life.

Mike Von Erich, 21, talked to reporters Monday for the first time since August 28, when he was admitted to Baylor University Medical Center with toxic shock syndrome.

The Dallas wrestler developed the rare staph infection after undergoing surgery August 22 at the Morton Cancer and Research Hospital in Dallas to repair a dislocated shoulder. His body temperature soared to nearly 107 degrees, and his blood pressure dropped dramatically, impairing his lungs, kidneys, heart, and other organs. He appeared to have little hope of surviving. His doctor calls his recovery remarkable. His family calls it a miracle.

"Mike has made a remarkable improvement," said Dr. William Sutker, an infectious disease specialist who has been caring for Mike since the wrestler developed toxic shock syndrome.

"He is no longer on dialysis," Sutker said at a news conference Monday. "We have stopped his intravenous feedings, because he is able to tolerate food by mouth. He has been out of his room and touring the hospital. There is no reason to suggest he cannot make a complete recovery."

Mike Von Erich, clad in pajamas and a robe, seconded his doctor's opinion. "I know I will be back," said Mike Von Erich, who was flanked by his brothers Kevin, Kerry, and Chris. "I cannot wait until the Cotton Bowl (an October 6 meet at which his brothers will wrestle). I am going to be there."

Mike said he hopes to leave Baylor this weekend, but he will only be able to watch the wrestling in the Cotton Bowl. He is probably months away from participating in a wrestling match, Sutker said.

A bandage on Mike's right foot covered the place where doctors had hooked him to a kidney-dialysis machine. His right eye was red from pink eye and a hemorrhage. A sling supported his left arm because he cannot yet rotate the shoulder on which he had surgery.

Still Mike said, "I feel good, really good. I have a lot of physical therapy. She comes in about twice a day."

When asked if he has resumed weight training for wrestling, Von Erich smiled and said, "I feel like it, but I cannot do it just yet."

Sutker said Von Erich, whose real name is Adkisson, would have to rebuild his strength gradually. Since Mike was admitted to Baylor, his weight dropped from 195 to 148, Sutker said.

"Healing is a progressive program of increasing physical therapy," Sutker said. "We are looking at months of recovery from a physical therapy standpoint." Besides physical therapy, Mike keeps busy opening the 3,000-plus pieces of mail he has received since entering Baylor.

The hospital had ordered only 650 thank-you notes to respond to all the fans' good wishes, said Jennifer Coleman, director of public relations. "We still get around-the-clock phone calls," she said, and urged fans to monitor news reports of Von Erich's condition instead of calling Baylor. Mike was released from Baylor University Medical Center on Friday, September 27, 1985, one month after he was *admitted. Once he was out he had one thing on his mind, and that was getting back in the ring where he said he belonged.*

******

As the days and months passed, I watched Mike try harder than I had ever seen anyone try to recover from an injury. However, his body was still very weak from his bout with toxic shock. I called Kevin and Kerry into my office one day and had a talk with them about Mike's progress. They told me they thought Mike was trying too hard. "He's like a person possessed," Kevin said. "Kerry and I have tried to get him to slow down but he insists that he is all right and that he will be back in the ring in a few months."

Mike was pushing himself to the limit and relying on prescription painkillers to help him make it through his daily physical exercises. He also started drinking alcohol a little more than usual. At one point I sat Mike down and he and I had a long talk. I told Mike that he had to quit taking so many pain pills; I tried to explain to him that relying on pills to help him through his exercises would sooner or later catch up to him and cause him more problems than he already had. Mike told me that he was aware that he was relying too much on medicine and would start cutting back.

Now, as I sit here telling you this story and thinking back on the way things were after Mike got out of the hospital, I should have stepped in and tried to help him more. I should have done something, anything! But how do you tell your son—who you almost lost and who has his heart and soul in something—that you think it is a bad idea? Our whole family stayed close to Mike for months, all of us watching him very carefully. We all tried to tell him that his health was more important than getting back in the ring, but he did not seem to hear us.

Meanwhile, friends and fans would say, "Hey Mike, how you feeling? When you going to start wrestling again?" The press would call the house to talk to Mike and ask the same questions. It seemed like the questions about when he would wrestle again made Mike more determined than ever to climb back into the ring. Doris and I felt so helpless, unable to change Mike's mind and not really sure at all how to handle the situation.

******

WRESTLER MIKE VON ERICH LEAVES HOSPITAL 1 DAY AFTER CAR ACCIDENT

Published, November 19, 1985

Wrestler Mike Von Erich of Grapevine was released late Monday evening from Lewisville Memorial Hospital after suffering a minor head injury in a one-car accident early Sunday, hospital officials said.

Mike Von Erich, 21, was removed from intensive care Monday morning, hospital officials said. His condition continued to improve throughout the day and he was listed in fair but stable condition just prior to his release at 5:30 p.m. Von Erich apparently lost control of his late model Lincoln Continental on State Highway 121 in Denton County Sunday morning and struck a parked car. Von Erich's car rolled over once, and he was either thrown through the sunroof or escaped through a broken window, Lewisville police said.

******

Mike continued to work out more and more until the day came when he insisted he was ready to step back in the ring. It did not seem to matter to Mike that the family did not feel he was ready. Mike had convinced the doctors that he was in the best shape of his life and he was going back into the ring with or without their approval. So on July 4, 1986, he got his chance at Reunion Arena. The match was a success.

******

MIKE VON ERICH'S RETURN IS VICTORIOUS— Fans cheer return of wrestler who almost lost his life last summer

By: Kevin B. Blackistone
Published, July 5, 1986

Jannette Baker waited for July 4 with special anticipation. Her parents were taking her to Reunion Arena to see the return of Mike Von Erich—the member of the wrestling Von Erich family who last August nearly lost his life in a bout with toxic shock syndrome.

Mike, the youngest of the four Von Erich wrestlers, suffered the infection after an operation for a separated shoulder from a match last summer.

"I was watching it on television when Mike got hurt," Jannette said. "I did not like it too well."

The 10-year-old Jannette said she mailed a get-well card to Mike Von Erich and prayed every night for his recovery.

"I have 29 pictures of the Von Erichs on my (bedroom) wall," she said. "I have a diary of them and all the newspaper clippings and programs and ticket stubs from the Von Erich matches I have been to." Friday night, she and her parents were among nearly 10,000 people who bought Texas flags and Von Erich pictures and T-shirts to the arena.

Shortly after 10:00 p.m. Friday, the music played, the spotlights shone and there was a roar from the crowds.

First came Kevin and Lance Von Erich. Then came the announcement:

"Ladies and gentlemen, this man came as close to death as humanly possible," said the ring announcer. "But thanks to the work of (doctors)…and the constant prayers and support from the wrestling fans all over the world and the Dallas, Fort Worth area, the World Class Wrestling Association introduces Mike Von Erich." And out came Mike.

The three were poised to retain their World Six-Man Tag-team championship against a trio of toughs named Hacksaw Butch Reed, Mad Dog Buzz Sawyer, and Matt Borne.

To the cheers of their fans, Mike entered the ring first and dropped Hacksaw Butch Reed with a flying drop kick. Mike rose and his brother Kevin jumped into the ring and raised Mike's right arm in the air to signify his hiatus was over.

In addition, less than 10 minutes later the trio of challengers were beaten and the Von Erich's were champions again.

"It is a miracle to have him back, period," Kevin said after the bout. "But to have him back in such top physical condition is just great."

"Physically, I have been training hard for four months," said a sweating but healthy Mike.

******

Jannette was especially happy. After the match, she was seeking an autograph for a special sketch of the Von Erich's she had brought from home.

The whole family was so glad to see Mike wrestling and finally happy again. At least, he seemed happy. But Doris kept saying she still felt that Mike just did not seem right in so many ways. He was prone to deep depressions, a problem I just did not pay enough attention to at the time. Looking back at things now, I guess I was blinded by the fact that the boys were doing well, and on the surface things seemed to be back to the way they were. Nonetheless, many small problems kept showing up in Mike's life.

Mike seemed to be having memory problems at times and trouble paying attention to things around him. He wrecked three cars in a matter of several months, and the whole family was starting to worry about his welfare. At times, he would sit and stare into space, and when someone would say something to him, he would start talking as if everything was fine. He was working out hard every day and would get upset if anyone told him to slow down.

Doris was worried about these changes in Mike and would tell the doctors this when she could speak to them alone. But the doctors just told her that those things were to be expected; after all that Mike had been through, we had to give him some more time to heal on his own.

******

WRESTLER PLEADS INNOCENT—MIKE VON ERICH DENIES ASSAULT CHARGES

By: Nita Thurman / Denton Bureau of the *News*
Published, February 4, 1987

> Denton—Mike Von Erich, a member of the wrestling Von Erich family, pleaded innocent Tuesday to a misdemeanor charge of assaulting a doctor at the Lewisville hospital in 1985.
>
> The wrestler, whose real name is Michael Brett Adkisson, is accused of striking a doctor May 30, 1985, when he went to an emergency room at First Texas Medical Center in Lewisville for treatment of an injured shoulder.
>
> In an opening statement during the first day of his trial before a six-person jury in Denton County Court-at-law No. 2, defense attorney Jerry Loftin said Von Erich "inadvertently" hit the doctor after the physician threatened to kick him out of the hospital and punched Von Erich on his injured shoulder.

His client was in a wheelchair and had one arm tied down in a shoulder immobilizer, Loftin said.

Prosecutor Jim Crouch told the jury he would present evidence that Von Erich was insulting and abusive to emergency room personnel and struck Dr. Timothy Shepherd in the face when the doctor tried to calm him down.

Shepherd sustained a fracture and damage to two teeth, Crouch said.

A class A misdemeanor assault charge carries a maximum penalty of a $1,000 fine and a year in the county jail.

The wrestler, who made his return to the ring in July 1986 at Reunion Arena in Dallas, is one of the three sons of the popular wrestling family headed by his father, Fritz Von Erich, whose real name is Jack Adkisson.

Both defense and prosecuting attorneys agree that Mike Von Erich was in extreme pain when he went to the emergency room, where he been treated previously for a shoulder separation. Loftin conceded that Von Erich made an insulting remark to a nurse.

"He waited 30 minutes, and he made the mistake of complaining," Loftin said.

Crouch said Von Erich cursed the nurse and upset other patients in the waiting room.

******

MIKE VON ERICH'S MOTHER TESTIFIES ON HIS SHOULDER PAIN BEFORE ASSAULT

By: Nita Thurman / Denton Bureau of the News
Published, February 7, 1987

Denton—the mother of wrestler Mike Von Erich testified Friday that a dislocated shoulder had kept her son in extreme pain for four days before he slugged a Lewisville doctor and was charged with assault. The wrestler's mother, Doris Adkisson, was the first witness called by defense attorney Jerry Loftin after state prosecutors on Friday afternoon rested their case against Von Erich. She is expected to resume testimony Monday morning.

Loftin contends the doctor punched Mike Von Erich on his injured shoulder before the wrestler hit the physician.

Mrs. Adkisson said she came to Denton from Tyler on May 26, 1985, after her son dislocated his shoulder. She went with him and his wife to Westgate Hospital in Denton that evening and to the Lewisville hospital the next day for pain shots, she said. "I have always been the head nurse in my family," she said.

As the wife of retired wrestler Fritz Von Erich and the mother of three wrestling sons, Mrs. Adkisson said, she is familiar with dislocated shoulders.

"It is extremely painful. It is unbearable when it (the shoulder joint) is completely out," she said.

******

On April 10, 1987, Mike became extremely depressed after being stopped by a police officer and taken to jail overnight on a DWI charge and possession of a controlled substance, a misdemeanor with less than 2 ounces of marijuana. When he left the jail he disappeared by himself and was never seen alive again.

Mike drove his car to an isolated park near Lake Lewisville, hiked several hundred yards into the brush, got into a sleeping bag, and ended his life with an overdose of sleeping pills. A Fort Worth doctor who was treating Mike's condition had prescribed the pills because of Mike's restlessness and inability to sleep.

A short note Mike left behind said, among other things, that he was going to a better place and that his brothers Jack Jr. and David would be waiting there for him, and for us not to worry.

Once again, the Von Erich family had been hit by death. Once again, another son was snatched; a brother buried.

******

'FAMILY' OF FANS ATTENDS FUNERAL FOR MIKE VON ERICH

By: Lori Stahl, Curtis Rist
Published, April 18, 1987

Whether dressed up or down—in shorts and T-shirts as though to watch a pro-wrestling match—the mourners at Mike Von Erich's wake Friday were not curiosity seekers. Their grief for the wrestler was real.

Fans—some for as long as 20 years—brought cards and flowers to a young man they felt they knew, someone they regarded as family.

"I wanted to come here because I really cared about Mike—he was a special part of my life," said Andrea Campbell, 18. She said that although she had only seen Mike Von Erich at matches and in crowded personal appearances, she felt a strong connection to the family.

"I moved here just after the first Von Erich memorial (David's) and I have been in it ever since," she said. David Von Erich died of an intestinal inflammation while touring Japan three years ago.

Many of the more than 400 mourners who viewed the closed casket at a funeral home in Lewisville expressed shock at the apparent suicide of the 23-year-old wrestler, whose body was found lying in a wooded area near Lewisville Lake Park Thursday.

Mike Von Erich died of a lethal dose of the tranquilizer Placidyl, Denton County Justice of the Peace Hubert H. Cunningham said Friday.

Cunningham said the Dallas County medical examiner's office determined that Mike Von Erich ingested and died from the slow-working substance sometime Sunday.

The details of his death made no difference to the Von Erich fans Friday afternoon. "We have been watching them so long, it feels like they're family," said Nancy Bardwell of Cleburne, who came to the wake with her daughter Darla, 12. Ms. Bardwell said that she had posters, T-shirts and 3 photo albums of Von Erich mementos. "It is not worth watching if it does not have a Von Erich in it," she said. "They are nice, friendly, and good Christians. They liked to help people.

"We just want the family to know we really care," she said. "We will miss him a lot." Although many of the fans hoped to console the members of the immediate family, only Von Erich's mother, Doris Adkisson, was at the funeral home during the public viewing hours. She did not greet the crowd, but a family friend, Tom Pulley, explained why other family members were not present. "The boys have always felt that they wanted to remember them the way they were, not the way they appear here," he said.

Kevin Von Erich did make a scheduled appearance at the Sportatorium Friday night, although he did not wrestle as originally planned.

As the event began Friday, David Manning, a former referee and a long-time associate of the Von Erich family, took to the ring and asked for a moment of silence from the fans in the half-filled arena.

"If there is a wrestling team in heaven," Manning said, "Mike Von Erich and his brother David will definitely be tag-team champions there."

After Manning spoke, Kevin Von Erich muscled through a group of people standing in one of the aisles and hopped into the ring. Fans pressed against one side of the ring and poked programs through the ropes for him to sign.

However, Kevin Von Erich, dressed in a black suit, was not there to wrestle or to please the fans.

"I am sure you will understand why I will not be wrestling," Kevin Von Erich said, as he paced the ring. "I have my priorities, and my priorities are with my mother and my family." Kevin said he would meet Nord the Barbarian, his scheduled opponent, at the fourth annual David Von Erich Memorial at Texas Stadium on May 4. He said that the event would also be dedicated to Mike.

Fans at the Sportatorium bought buttons, posters, and photographs of the bare-chested Mike Von Erich before taking their seats in the half-filled arena. Some clutched copies of newspapers with front-page accounts of the wrestler's death.

Kathy Fell, a 21-year-old Arlington office worker, bought a color poster of Mike Von Erich for her sister, Jami, 14, of Krum. They had gone to many of the weekly matches at the Sportatorium and Jami had been acquainted with the wrestler.

While waiting for the match to start—and wondering if Kevin Von Erich would go ahead and wrestle as scheduled—the two talked about Mike, whom they knew personally. "He was so alive and always talked to his fans," Miss Fell said. "He used to call Jami up and talk to her over the phone."

Jami Fell said she used to bring a yellow carnation to every match she attended. On Thursday, the two women sent the family a $50 bouquet of yellow carnations.

This faith is the reason the Von Erich family has withstood the incredible trauma death has thrown at them. Again and again and again. A pain that would crush weaker individuals, a sadness only a mother, father, or brother can feel. They have vowed to continue despite their horrible setbacks.

******

As Doris and I stood frozen at Mike's graveside, we were comforted by our faith that it would be only a temporary separation. Mike was with Jack Jr. and David, and someday our entire family would be together again in the arms of the Lord. Nonetheless, I could not stop myself from questioning my faith in the Lord again, asking why yet another one of my sons had to die at such an early age. This was more than any one family deserved and I knew in the bottom of my heart that my faith in God was starting to fade. Once again, I started wondering if the Lord was out there and why he felt the need for my family and I to suffer yet another loss of a family member that we all loved so very much. I had also begun to wonder if the Von Erich family was cursed—a question that I would come to ask myself many times in the future.

I had started taking care of a lot of the Sportatorium business again to keep my mind off my sons' deaths. And again I was starting to have problems in my business dealings, and in the mornings it was getting harder and harder to get out of bed knowing that I had to go to the Sportatorium for business as usual. I had gotten to the point where I did not even like to think or hear about wrestling. I finally decided to get totally out of the wrestling business after the doctors told me I was worrying too much. I no longer wanted anything to do with wrestling ever again. I felt that wrestling had cost me too much in the way of three sons, so I turned World Class Championship Wrestling over to Kevin and Kerry and sold all my other wrestling interests, and to this day I have never had anything to do with the wrestling business since.

******

Mike won the following titles in his short, four-year career:

WCCW SIX-MAN TAG-TEAM TITLE

05/06/1984—with Fritz and Kevin Von Erich (Fritz came out of retirement to replace Kerry, so Kerry could meet Rick Flair for the world championship).
09/03/1984—with Kevin and Kerry Von Erich
12/31/1984—with Kevin and Kerry Von Erich
07/03/1986—with Kevin and Lance Von Erich

NWA AMERICAN HEAVYWEIGHT TITLE

08/04/1984—Mike Von Erich defeats Gino Hernandez for the title

WORLD CLASS MIDDLE EAST HEAVYWEIGHT TITLE

08/07/1985—Mike Von Erich wins

CHAPTER 10

Chris was the youngest of my boys and had by far the best personality. He was one of those kids who were always smiling and making friends wherever they went; people would become friends with Chris from the moment they met him. Chris always had a lot of friends while he was growing up, but his best buddy in the whole world was his brother Mike, even though the age difference between the two boys was greater than the age difference between the older boys. Mike seemed to take care of his little brother and would always be there for him if the time ever arose.

Mike taught himself to play the guitar, and at the same time Chris learned the drums. The two of them would frequently jam together. Sometimes, when their enthusiasm would get the better of them and the music got really loud, the neighbors would call the police. But nobody could stay mad at Chris for long. When the police would arrive Chris would answer the door, invite the officers in, and the next thing you knew they would be joining in. Then, the next day, Chris would go over to the neighbor's house and apologize for making so much noise and ask them if there was any way he and Mike could make up for it.

Chris, like Kerry, was one of the family's better practical jokers. When Chris was a teenager he could get away with almost all his little jokes he was constantly playing on the entire family, even though his winning smile and wide eyes were usually a clue that Chris was up to no good. He was always pulling some type of joke on Kevin and Kerry, and the three of them kept trying to one-up each other with their practical jokes. Later, after Mike got into wrestling, we had all kinds of problems with Chris and school because he would want to blow off his schoolwork and hang out with his brothers.

Chris grew up going to the Sportatorium and watching me and his brothers wrestle. He was always helping all of us in any way he could. From an early age he was involved in the wrestling business in some way or another. Chris would beg his brothers to take him along on wrestling trips and would get very upset at his mother and me if we said no. He always had a sunny disposition, but his personality took on a very big change after Mike passed away. Losing his brother Mike hurt that boy more than anyone could ever know. After Mike's funeral, Chris kept to himself for months. The practical jokes came to a stop and the sunny smile disappeared. Chris had started to change, sometimes getting upset over the smallest things. He started staying away from home more than usual, and his mother and I were starting to suspect drug and alcohol abuse.

Chris loved anything having to do with American Indians. He was always looking for arrowheads and reading books about the different tribes throughout the United States, and had many Indian artifacts in his room. He was much like his other brothers and me, because he loved hunting, fishing, and just being out in the open spaces. Chris had read a book about the sacred Indian praying circle, a special place where warriors would go to be alone with their thoughts of upcoming battles. Chris had built his own Indian praying circle near our house in East Texas. The circle had been built from rocks that Chris had spent years collecting from different Indian sites he had visited throughout Texas and Oklahoma. He had started working on his circle when we first moved out to East Texas and would add rocks and other artifacts to it for years, and it became his favorite place to go when he wanted to be alone.

One day, after Chris had been sitting in the praying circle, he came into the house and announced to his mother and me that he was going into pro-wrestling, to take Mike's place. Doris and I just looked at each other, not knowing what to say. Chris had suffered from serious asthma problems since early childhood and the asthma medicine he had taken all his life had stunted his growth and left him with very brittle bones. We did not think wrestling was a good idea and we tried very hard to talk him out of it. Even Kevin and Kerry agreed with us and did their best to help talk Chris out of a wrestling career.

But Chris had already made up his mind that he was going to take his brother Mike's place in the ring. Chris had once jumped in the ring and hit one of the Freebirds, Buddy Roberts, in the back of the head with a chair because Roberts had hit Mike from behind with a foreign object. I have always thought that Chris had it in his head that since Mike had taken David's place in the six-man tag team match; he was supposed to take Mike's place in the ring.

All his life Chris had wanted to be a wrestler like his father and brothers. When he was very young Doris and I tried to get him interested in something besides wrestling, but he could not be distracted from his goal. He insisted on going to wrestling school when he was young, and if he could not be at the matches in person, he would be sitting on the floor watching them on TV in his room.

Chris trained very hard for several months, running for miles each day and lifting weights until all hours of the morning, and although Kevin and Kerry kept putting off getting Chris a real match, the night finally came when Chris entered the ring as a professional wrestler. Well, poor Chris broke his arm that night in his very first match tagging with his brother Kevin. His bones were just too brittle to be in the ring.

After that night, Chris went on to wrestle a few more matches, and I think he got hurt in almost every one of them. He began to get depressed and I suspected drug use more than ever. His mother and I would try very hard to talk to him and try to find out what was going on in that boy's head, but he would never talk to us that much and never about the deaths of his brothers. I never thought Chris would take his own life because he seemed to be such a happy young man growing up. I have always felt that when Chris realized he would never be able to replace his brother Mike in the ring, it was too much for him to bear. He must have felt that he had let his family and all the Von Erich fans down.

******

The following interview appeared in *The Wrestler Magazine* in October 1990 after Chris's first pro-match with Percy Pringle:

Q & A with Chris Von Erich
From: *The Wrestler*
October 1990

Q: Chris, congratulations on your very impressive debut. It looks like you'll be the answer to a trivia question from now on.

A: Really? What question is that? Let me guess—who was the fifth Von Erich brother to wrestle?

Q: That's true, but I had something else in mind. When Mike (Von Erich) had his first match in 1984, he made his wrestling debut against General Skandar Akbar. Now you've had your first match against a manager as well.

A: That's pretty interesting. Hey, if I turn out to be half the wrestler that any of my brothers have been, then I will be a very proud young man. But I think that it's important to keep my ring debut in a proper perspective.

Q: What do you mean?

A: Well, when I made the challenge to Percy Pringle, I didn't do it because I had some grandiose idea about rocketing to the top of the USWA ratings or anything like that. I did it to prove a point. Both Percy Pringle and Matt Borne turned against Kerry and Kevin, and one way they got their point across was by attacking me. Once again, I felt like I had gotten in my brother's way, you know. It seems like whenever I get near a ring, trouble starts—and I couldn't do anything to help out, which really made me upset.

Q: The fans were upset when Borne blindsided you. He just lifted you up and rammed you headfirst into the ring apron as hard as he could. It really looked like you might have been hurt very badly.

A: Yeah, I had a pretty bad headache for about five days. But what felt worse was that everybody was running around saying, "Poor little Chris Von Erich." Little Chris this…Little Chris that. People around here have always treated me like I'm 10 years old or something. Hey, I'm a man. I'm 20 years old now, and I figured it was about time to stand up for myself.

Q: And that's why you challenged Percy Pringle?

A: Exactly. Granted, I couldn't really do much against Matt Borne. He's about twice my size, and if I ever wrestled him he'd probably take my head off. So if I couldn't get my revenge on Matt, the next best thing would be to polish off his shady manager. So that's what I did, and believe me, I feel really good about it. It was so nice to finally get up in the ring and show the world that while I may not be the biggest guy in the world, at least I can hold my own with a lying sack of manure like Pringle. I'll tell you, when I hit him in the belly, it was just like sticking my hand in my mama's sourdough bread before she sticks it in the oven. What a slob!

Q: So this makes your record 1-0 as a pro. What are your future plans as far as getting in the ring goes?

A: I really don't know at this point. After I beat him, Pringle kept going around saying that my pinfall was a fluke, that he could beat me if I wrestled him again. I might just do that. Hey, it's fun putting some knots in his fat head, so if he's dumb enough to want to make a hobby out of it, then it's fine with me.

Q: But how about wrestling against other wrestlers?

A: (Pauses) That's a question that I'll really have to put a lot of thought into. Kevin and Kerry have been everything I could ask for and more during my training. For years, they have taken time out of their busy schedules to work out with me in the gym, and they showed me holds, maneuvers, and all the training techniques you could shake a stick at. Right now, I'd bet that I know more about wrestling than half of the active competitors out there. But, well, I'm…gee, how do I put this?

Q: Don't be ashamed, Chris. It's obvious to everyone that you're a bit on the small side.

A: (Sheepishly) There, you said it for me. That's right. I am small. After working out for years, I've managed to build my body to about 200 pounds. But I still can't change the fact that I'm barely 5'7". There's nothing that I can do about that. So, unless the USWA decides to sanction a light heavyweight division, there's no way I could compete against some of the bruisers that are around here. Could you imagine me against Jeff Gaylord? Or Mike Awesome? I'd get my head handed to me on a plate!

Q: That's probably true. But not every wrestler is a giant. Look at Bill Dundee. He's only 5'7", but he held the USWA Southwestern belt twice, and that's only one of the many titles he's won.

A: Yeah, I know that. Dundee is a role model for many of us who've been told that we're too small to be athletes. I've talked with Jeff Jarrett about that, too. However, right now I think it is important to pick and choose my sports. Am I going to become a full-time professional wrestler? I think the answer to that question is no. Will I ever wrestle again? The answer to that question, though, is an emphatic yes. I think there will be plenty of opportunities to help my brothers in the future. Maybe I can give an assist in six-man tag team matches. Or maybe they'll just need somebody to hang out at ringside to look for Pringle or Akbar. Whenever I'm needed, you can bet I'll be there.

Q: It looks as if Kerry and Kevin will no doubt need your help. On the same card in which you made your debut, Kevin wrestled Borne and defeated him by disqualification. But after the match, Gary Young ran out and cut Kevin's hair with scissors that were handed to him by Terrance Garvin.

A: You see the problem here? All the time, people gang up on each other in the USWA. That's the influence of that rat Akbar. As long as he's around as a manager, wrestlers are going to try to break the rules—particularly where my brothers are concerned. Now Kevin looks terrible because Young hacked off some of his hair. Well, the biggest thing that daddy always taught me is that I should always look out for my brothers. I just wish that I could've been there at that point. I think I'm more than man enough to take care of a prancing screamer like Garvin!

Q: You've brought up an interesting idea. Since you've been so successful against Pringle, how about taking on the USWA's other rule—breaking managers? After watching you in action against Percy, you might just have a shot at defeating Akbar.

A: That's an intriguing thought. We could even put some special stipulations on the bout. We could make it loser leaves the USWA. Hey, if I lost, then I probably don't deserve to be a pro wrestler anyway. But if I won, I'd be the biggest USWA hero since Eric Embry last year. (Laughs) Who knows? Maybe we can sign a match like that real soon. I doubt that coward Akbar would go for it, though.

Q: Things are certainly starting to look up for the Von Erich's. Kerry is riding high as the Texas champion, Kevin is starting to get into the action full-time again, and you've made your successful debut. What do you hope to see happen in the future?

A: For myself, I just want to remain healthy and happy. But I want nothing but the best for my brothers. Kerry seems very happy with the Texas belt, so I hope he can hold that for as long as he wants. Kevin has designs on the USWA title, for sure. What I'd like to see is for both of them to be champions. That would make me very proud.

Q: I've talked to both Kevin and Kerry since your debut victory and they both said that they're very proud of you.

A: I don't think I could ever ask for more.

******

That article shows exactly what I mean about Chris. That boy wanted nothing more from life than to be just like his dad and his brothers. If Chris had been a little bit bigger and had not had all those medical problems, I think he would have been just as good a wrestler as his brothers and me.

In my opinion, what Chris had to go though in his life— being too small and all, and trying to make it in a sport that is almost totally dominated by big guys—was a hard thing for a boy to have to go through. My opinion of Chris has always been very high. He tried so hard to overcome an impossible handicap, and he had more heart than all the other Von Eriches put together. Chris killed himself less than a year after that interview with *The Wrestler Magazine* was taken. Doris and Kevin found Chris's body out at that Indian praying circle he spent so much time at. It was around nine at night and he had a 9mm pistol by his side. He had shot himself in the head. Chris had not given anyone a clue that he was thinking about taking his own life; in fact, I had just talked to him earlier that morning and he seemed in a really good mood.

Chris had left a suicide note. It just said he was very sorry for what he felt he had to do and that he loved his mother, me, Kevin, and Kerry, and was going to be with his other brothers in heaven. When I found out what had happened, I became very numb and sick to my stomach. I no longer knew what to say or think. I sat down and cried for hours in my room before I could pull myself together and face my family.

While I was searching the Internet one day I came across a website dedicated to Chris Von Erich. As I looked through the site, I was very touched by the words I read. The girls who had designed that webpage, Jenny and Connie, were very dedicated Chris Von Erich fans and their words tell their feeling. After e-mailing Jenny, she and I became good friends, so I thought I would add the following tributes and poetry dedicated to Chris from these girls.

******

Tributes and Poetry
Dedicated To
Chris Von Erich

CHRIS VON ERICH A Texas Sweetheart

By:
—Jenny—

I was asked to do one of the most difficult things I think I've ever had to do: put my feelings for Chris Von Erich to paper. Not knowing him personally, they aren't normal feeling that one might have for a friend or even a brother. However, they are feelings just the same.

Living in Michigan, exposure to the Von Eriches was minimal. But ESPN began showing USWA wrestling for one hour at 4:00 p.m. each weekday. Each day, after school, I had the television on—I ruled that set for one hour. This was my first glimpse of Chris Von Erich. Being a teenager, the first thing that attracted me to Chris was his looks. He had that little boy charm and an all-around sweet disposition about him. Until then, Jeff Jarrett had been my favorite. And while I still liked him, Chris was quickly wrestling his way into my heart. Unfortunately, he wasn't televised often, but the more I saw of him the more I realized that he was more than good looks and pretty eyes. Chris Adkisson had heart and he had guts. He worked his way into a world made for big men. He didn't let his small stature hold him back. He was the type of man who warranted respect—and while most were critical of him, I kept in mind that many people wouldn't have even tried. Right there, that made him golden.

I only have two matches on tape, a few magazine interviews, and a few pictures. Memories are what keep him alive. I've had the chance to chat with Ms. Doris, Chris's Mom, and I found out things I never knew about him. Like his favorite color. That he liked to draw, pet names. He was really into Indians. The things that made Chris what he was. Chris made me believe in him, in the Von Erich name. My one dream had been to meet him, to tell him what a fan I was, and how I believed in him. I never got that chance, but now I feel I have been given a chance. Chris was a fighter, a man, and a champion. He didn't have a gimmick or a catchy-sounding name. The beautiful styled robes he donned for his walk to the ring were the only "flashy" parts of his image. In the ring, he had the basic trunks and boots. The one thing I remember the most is how his socks used to stick up above the boots. He had that "go out there and be the best I can" air about him, and in my opinion, he did just that. Tragedy took Chris from his family, friends, and fans. That is what most people remember about him. No one knew his favorite color was blue. No one knew that he once had a snake named Fluffy. Let us remember Chris Barton Adkisson (Von Erich) as a human, with a sense of humor and a kind heart. I hope I was able to convey my feelings for Chris, but to be honest this doesn't do him justice. Nor could I never find the words to do so. My one hope is that he is at peace and knows he touched someone. Someone who will never forget the name, Chris Von Erich. To me, he was a champion—and he didn't need a gold belt to show me that.

LEFT OVER
By:
—M—

Your emotional trespass of placidity,
Enslaving a depressed existence,
To take up arms against yourself,
But you didn't kill the demons,
Such a beautiful shell
Was grotesquely filled,
Consuming pain in Angelic eyes,

The terrors of your visions,
What were you thinking?
With the lead to your head?
Were your tears only for yourself ?

In zealous convictions you now see as Lies,
But to turn back now shows weakness,

So, you've blown it away in bits of gray,
Exchanging despondence for Death's Ardor,
Yet sympathy remains for you,
A life lived in smoke and mirrors,
An inheritance starving for Fame,
Fed on cold empathetic Left Over's.

SAPPHIRE REQUIEM

By:

—Mickie—

An enameled, cerulean bowl of sky steals my attention for a moment,
A chill in the air belies the brilliance of the sunlight,
The day seems to be filled with a shrouded vacancy,
As with a solar eclipse or a moonless night,
Something (someone?) brighter is missing.
Mid-September finds me shivering.
Indigo eyes, which radiated warmth and stirred souls,
Puckish humor dancing with unaffected compassion,
A soaring, windswept spirit who was never too proud to help some-one,
The stains of inferiority were only a treacherous mirage in a desert of desperation,
Their stings more poisonous than that of any scorpion,
You are not forgotten, sweet courageous son of the earth,
No eclipse is permanent,
The moon ultimately rejoins the heavens,
Even the most distant tide finally returns to the shore,
Kindness never truly dies,
And you shall always have a home in our hearts.

News articles were taken from the *Dallas Morning News* Archives: All articles are printed as they appeared.

YOUNGEST VON ERICH WRESTLER DIES AFTER GUNSHOT TO HEAD

By: Associated Press
Published, September 13, 1991

TYLER, Texas—Chris Adkisson, the youngest of the ill-fated Von Erich family of professional wrestlers, died Thursday night after being hospitalized with a gunshot wound to the head, officials said.

ADULATION GIVEN TO DAD, SIBLINGS ELUDED YOUNGEST OF VON ERICHS

By: Todd J. Gillman, Mitch Lawrence / staff writer for the *Dallas Morning News* Published, September 14, 1991

On a Thursday night last month, Chris Adkisson spent three hours signing autographs for wrestling fans at Kowbell Indoor Rodeo in Mansfield.

It was not a large gig for a member of the star-crossed Von Erich wrestling dynasty, whose patriarch, Fritz Von Erich, built an international television wrestling empire around Chris' older brothers. The youngest and by far the smallest of the family's wrestlers, the adoration that followed his brothers and father seemed to elude him.

He apparently committed suicide late Thursday, authorities said, and was the fourth of six Von Erich sons to die young. His brother, Kevin, and their mother, Doris, found the 21-year-old a hundred yards north of their East Texas ranch house, a 9mm pistol beside him.

The Van Zandt County Sheriff's Department said Mr. Adkisson shot himself in the head and was pronounced dead at 10:27 p.m. at East Texas Medical Center in Tyler. Investigators found a suicide note, whose contents were not released.

"How in the world can you just keep burying one son after another? I cannot imagine how heartbreaking it must be, to lose one child after another," said Norma Shotts, a neighbor who lives outside Edom, a small town about 80 miles east of Dallas.

Several people who knew Chris, who reportedly was only 5-feet 5-inches tall, noted the intense pressure he faced to enter wrestling.

"They were to wrestling probably what the Kennedys were to the White House," said Stan Hovatter Jr., who did public relations for the Von Erichs in 1986, as their popularity started to wane. "There was a certain image they gave off, like they were royalty."

He added, "I feel sorry for Chris. He was small…but he had the unbelievable reputation to live up to, with the family name. When you think about all that happened to the family, if he was suffering from some type of emotional trauma and problems, it is easy to understand why (he might have killed himself). How do you deal with the death of three brothers?"

Their father, Fritz Von Erich, told KLTV in Tyler on Friday that his youngest son wanted to follow in the family tradition. "I wanted my kids to go into a profession of some type, but because of me, I suppose, going with me to all of the matches…that is what they all wanted to be, including Chris."

Bill Mercer, a longtime wrestling broadcaster and family friend, said they were "unbelievable stars. There was a magic, a charisma, whatever it is…After David died it began to slip. Then Mike's illness and suicide. They were like a great shooting star that goes up and suddenly fades out," he said.

Justice of the peace Bill Lemmert in Tyler said he would not rule on a cause in Mr. Adkisson's death before receiving autopsy results, probably on Monday.

Friends and neighbors recalled the younger Adkisson as a friendly, outgoing boy who admired his brothers.

Despite severe asthma that hampered his athletic efforts, he sought to follow the family path into professional wrestling, they said.

David Meltzer, publisher of the Wrestling Observer, a national newsletter, said, "From the time he was born there was so much pressure to live up to the standards of Kevin, David, Kerry, and Mike. Chris could never be a superstar in wrestling. He was just too small.

"When you grow up, and your whole life you are groomed to be a champion wrestler, it has to be very hard when you physically cannot do it," he said.

Chris had only a few matches during his brief wrestling career. He did not win any titles.

CHAPTER 11

After Kerry won the National Wrestling Alliance World Heavyweight Championship belt from Ric Flair, it seemed like nothing could hold him back. His career was soaring. He loved the wrestling business and he loved his fans. His personal life was going well, too. In 1984, Kerry married, and by the following year he and his wife, Cathy, were expecting their first child.

Kerry lost his championship belt in a rematch with Flair a few months after he won it at Texas Stadium, but assured his fans he would win it back again in short order. Kerry got that chance on January 7, 1985, when he squared off against Flair at the Will Rogers Coliseum in Fort Worth.

******

News articles were taken from the *Dallas Morning News* archives: all articles are printed as they appeared.

TIME LIMIT THWARTS KERRY VON ERICH'S TITLE TRY

By: Stan Hovatter Jr. / Special to the *News*
Published, January 8, 1985

Mondays night's match for the National Wrestling Alliance world title was set just the way Kerry Von Erich wanted it.

Kerry Von Erich, the challenger from Denton, won a Christmas match with Ric Flair, the champ from Minnesota, but did not take the title because the belt cannot change hands on a disqualification. That rule was waived for Monday's rematch at Will Rogers Coliseum.

However, the 60-minute time limit was in effect. In addition, that, more than anything, got the better of Kerry Von Erich.

Flair and Von Erich wrestled to a draw in the time limit, allowing Flair to keep his title, which he will defend Friday night at the Sportatorium against Terry "Bam Bam" Gordy. "This fight has just begun, Flair," Kerry Von Erich told a capacity crowd of 8,000 after the match. "Let's go five more minutes."

In addition, there might have been at least five minutes left to wrestle. A ringside reporter timed the match at 52 minutes.

Could Kerry Von Erich have defeated Ric Flair with that extra time? "Yeah," said Von Erich. "I think so. I had him down for a long time in the end."

Kerry Von Erich pinned Flair for a 2-count 10 times in the past seven minutes. The last time came right before the bell; 30 seconds after Von Erich applied the Iron Claw to Flair's head. Von Erich, who used such moves as the backslide, sunset flip, figure-four leg lock and the suplex, had 16 pins for 2-counts to Ric Flair's 12. However, Von Erich only had control of the match in the last 10 minutes.

Von Erich said he was "physically ready but mentally not out there," after his pet dog was killed earlier in the day. "It really got to me," Von Erich said. "I guess you have to be a dog-lover to understand that."

Kerry really had life going his way. But things changed suddenly one day a few months after his brother Mike got out of the hospital following his bout with toxic shock syndrome. Kerry was on his motorcycle speeding toward his home in Roanoke, when a police car pulled out in front of him to make a left turn. Kerry hit the police car at a high rate of speed and was thrown off his motorcycle, over the car, and onto the high-way. The police did a very good job in stopping the flow of blood until a Care Flight helicopter could arrive and transport Kerry to Baylor Medical Center.

WRESTLER FAIR AFTER SURGERY— Pins put in ankle of Kerry Von Erich

By: Jan Crawford
Published, June 6, 1986

Popular Texas wrestler Kerry Von Erich was injured earlier this week when his motorcycle collided with a patrol car. Von Erich was listed in fair condition late Thursday after an almost four-hour operation at Baylor University Medical Center, physicians said.

Von Erich, 25, whose real name is Kerry Adkisson, sustained a fractured right ankle, dislocated right hip and a long cut on his right knee in the accident in southwest Denton County. Several pins and metal rods were placed in his fractured ankle, which will be put in a cast and later a brace, said Dr. Howard Moore, who performed the surgery. Moore refused to estimate how long Von Erich will be out of wrestling, saying he must undergo extensive rehabilitation, along with another operation to remove the pins and metal rods from his ankle.

Von Erich was headed to his home in Roanoke on Wednesday when he crashed into the back of an Argyle patrol car on State Highway 377. Von Erich was "pretty groggy" Thursday, said Fritz Von Erich, Kerry's father.

Fritz Von Erich, whose real name is Jack Adkisson, is the patriarch of Texas's most famous wrestling family.

He said it would not be long before his son returns to the ring.

"Kerry's life is not threatened," Fritz said. "Where the Lord's will is in this is what we will accept. Do not count old Kerry out, not by a long shot."

Kerry is one of four sons coached in the sport from childhood by his father, a one-time villain of the wrestling world.

And Fritz said another Von Erich, his son, Mike, will be back in the ring July 4 at Reunion Arena. Mike was hospitalized in September at Baylor in critical condition with toxic shock syndrome, a rare infection caused by a staph bacterium. The bacteria apparently entered Mike's body through a surgical incision made to repair a dislocated shoulder.

The Von Erich family have remained prominent figures in the wrestling world, partly because of their appeal to audiences—especially teen-age girls, said Bob Siegel, a long-time family friend and president of the National Wrestling Alliance. Siegel said Kerry Von Erich, ranked the No. 1 wrestler in the world by World Wrestling magazine, had added excitement and some legitimacy to the wrestling scene.

Baylor University Medical Center has been inundated with telephone calls from fans in support of Kerry Von Erich.

SURGERY REPAIRS WRESTLER'S FOOT—
Doctors optimistic that Von Erich will appear again in the ring

By: Jan Crawford
Published, June 10, 1986

Kerry Von Erich, a popular Texas wrestler injured last week in a motorcycle accident, was in fair condition Monday at Baylor Medical Center after a 15-hour operation Sunday to replace muscle and tissue in his right foot, hospital officials said.

Dr. William Sutker, Von Erich's attending physician, would not estimate when Kerry Von Erich will be back in the ring. However, he said, "Everyone is optimistic he will return."

Kerry Von Erich was injured Wednesday when the motorcycle he was driving struck an Argyle police patrol car in Denton County. Von Erich suffered a fractured right foot, a dislocated right hip and a long cut across his right knee. He had surgery Thursday to place pins and metal rods in his foot.

Von Erich was having a second operation Sunday to clean his wounds when doctors detected dead tissue and muscle fiber in his foot. They scheduled Sunday's operation to improve blood flow in his leg and prevent infection, Sutker said.

In the microscopic surgery Sunday, Drs. Frederick Lester and Steve Bird replaced the region of dead tissue in Von Erich's foot with muscle tissue from under his arm, Sutker said.

Habgood said Von Erich was alert and stable on Monday and has received hundreds of cards and letters from fans wishing him a speedy recovery.

Kerry Von Erich is ranked No. 1 wrestler in the world by *World Wrestling Magazine*. He returned last week to his home in Roanoke, Denton County, from a wrestling tour in Japan, where he won the All-Asian Championship title.

******

What happened in that motorcycle accident was that Kerry was speeding on a very busy Texas road as he went to pass a car. As he did, he did not see the police car, which had pulled into the left turn lane. Kerry hit the police car and went flying over the top of the car, catching his right foot and ankle on the police car's emergency lights, and hitting the hard payment some fifty feet away from the police car.

Kerry's foot was severed in the accident and he almost bled to death on the highway before the Care Flight helicopter could arrive. After being transported to Baylor Hospital in Dallas, it had taken doctors many hours of painstaking surgery to reattach Kerry's foot. Later, when Kerry was still in the hospital after over twenty hours of microsurgery, he got it in his mind that he wanted a cheeseburger. For some reason that Kerry was never quite able to explain to everyone, he got out of bed and walked down to the cafeteria to get his cheeseburger, and in the process messed his foot up so bad that the doctors had no choice but to remove it. When I asked Kerry why he had gotten out of bed and walked to the cafeteria, he replied that he did not think his foot was that bad and he was starving to death for something to eat; the nurses did not have time to get him a burger even after he had offered one nurse fifty dollars.

Losing his foot like to have killed Kerry, he loved wrestling so much and he was really scared his injury would mark the end of his career. He made everyone promise not to let the news out about his foot. Per his request, nobody knew he had lost his foot except the doctors, Kerry's family, and a few close friends.

Kerry was later fitted with a prosthetic foot about six weeks after being released from Baylor Medical Center. Once he had his prosthetic foot, he began the long and difficult task of learning to use it. He worked out constantly, determined to return to professional wrestling and never letting any of the many obstacles that he faced every day stand in his way.

Through sheer determination and months of hard work, Kerry did learn to wrestle with that prosthetic foot, but he would be in so much pain after a match that he could barely make it back to the dressing room by himself. Kerry began to take pain medication before and after every bout. It hurt the family to see Kerry this way, and we all sat down with him at one time or another to try to convince him to give up wrestling. He refused to even listen to that kind of talk. He and Kevin almost came to blows when Kevin suggested one day that Kerry find something else to do with his life.

In 1990, Kerry left Dallas due to the many arguments over him climbing back into the ring from friends and family. Kerry disappeared for a few months, not contacting any of the family, and later turned up wrestling for the WWF as the Texas Tornado. Kerry went on to win the World Wrestling Federation Intercontinental Championship title with a prosthetic foot, but the mental price he had to pay took its toll on Kerry. Just as with his younger brother Mike, severe psychological problems would haunt Kerry for many years afterward, leading to severe drug and alcohol abuse.

******

WRESTLER PLEADS NO CONTEST TO FRAUDULENTLY OBTAINING DRUGS

By: (?)
Published, August 5, 1992

Kerry Gene Adkisson, who wrestles professionally as Kerry Von Erich, pleaded no contest Tuesday in Dallas County Court to six counts of obtaining drugs with a false prescription.

The 32-year-old Mr. Adkisson, a member of the Von Erich wrestling family, chose not to defend himself against allegations that he fraudulently obtained Valium, Vicodin, and Didrex from pharmacies in Dallas County this year. He is to be sentenced on September 10, in State District Court. He could face up to 60 years in prison and up to $60,000 in fines.

On September 10, 1992, Kerry went back to court and received ten-year probation. He promised the court he would seek professional help for his pain pill addiction and agreed to community service.

******

I had hoped the court's decision would shock Kerry into getting off the pain medication, which would mean he would have to give up his career as a professional wrestler. There was no way he could stand the pain of fighting without painkillers. But Kerry was more determined than ever to stay a wrestler regardless of what it took.

As time went by, I did not see much of Kerry. He was wrestling for one promoter after another and traveling around a lot, so we did not have many chances to sit down and talk. I was aware that Kerry was starting to have problems with his marriage, but he kept his other problems to himself, refusing to sit down and talk to his family about the many problems in his life. It was much later that I would learn that those problems were getting bigger and bigger and that his drug and alcohol problems were completely out of control.

Most of the things that were going on with Kerry I would hear about from Kevin. Doris and I were having our own problems at that time. One day during dinner she stood up from the kitchen table and announced that she and I would be getting a divorce. That was the first I had heard about it, or anyone else in the family for that matter. We sold our dream house near Edom where Chris had shot himself and split everything that she and I owned in half. She went her way and I moved to the small house on the 150 acres that I still owned on Lake Dallas in Denton County. I have always loved that land. It was the first land that I ever owned and I would not give it up. I think that at one time or another all the boys lived in this little house when they were in college and had moved out of the house with me and their mom.

Around this time, Kerry was pulled over and arrested for possession of cocaine. He had been stopped in Dallas County after a warrant for his arrest had already been issued for forging prescriptions for pain pills. Since he had broken his probation, he was now facing jail time. He had just recently been divorced from his wife of nearly ten years and was in trouble with the IRS for back taxes along with Kevin. Less than a year after I turned the business over to Kevin and Kerry, they were forced to file for bankruptcy. Both Kevin and Kerry were great wrestlers, but neither of them had any idea how to run a business and would not ask me for help. Kerry had recently been fired from the World Wrestling Federation for failing a drug test and was having problems finding promoters who would hire him. So he really had nowhere to go but back to Dallas, where he and Kevin made a last effort to keep the Sportatorium operating.

On February 8, 1993, Kerry and his girlfriend pulled up at my house on Lake Dallas. I was out back working in my pepper garden when I saw them pull up to the house. Kerry got out of the car and waved to me as he went inside the house. A short while later, he came out of the house and got into the jeep that I keep for driving around on the property. He drove right by me without stopping and never even looked up at me. He had left his girlfriend sitting on the swing in the back of the house, so I walked up to her and asked if anything was wrong with Kerry. She said he had been very upset for the past few days and that he and Kevin had gotten in a bad argument on the phone just after midnight. Kerry had told her he had to go by his father's house and get something at the back of the 150 acres and for her to wait there until he returned.

I was thinking that the whole story sounded sort of strange and wondered if I should call Kevin and find out what was wrong. As I walked into the house to use the phone, I noticed one of the doors open on the cabinets where I kept a few handguns. All of a sudden, a strange feeling rushed over my body and I knew something was terribly wrong.

I got in my truck and drove all over the 150-acre property looking for Kerry. Years earlier, when Kerry had been in college, he had fixed up an old rundown house that was at the back of our property and lived there a couple of years. The roof on the house had fallen in years ago and was just rotting away.

I found the jeep parked in back of the house with Kerry nowhere in sight. I got out of the truck and began walking through the woods, calling his name.

I found Kerry sitting on the ground, his back against a tree and his head down, the gun he'd taken from the house still in his hand. He had shot himself through the heart with a .44 magnum handgun.

I sat down beside Kerry's body and started to cry, asking myself over and over why this had happened to another one of my beloved sons. I looked up to the heavens and renounced God forever that day. I screamed at the top of my lungs that God was not there and that I would never look toward the heavens for help in my life again. I felt in my heart that I was utterly alone. I sat there crying as I stared at the .44 magnum handgun still clutched in my dead son's hand, and considered using it on myself. A short time had passed and the idea of taking my own life faded away. I had my last few words with Kerry as I got up off the ground, and through my tears found my way back to my truck and drove back to the house and called the Sheriff's department.

******

VON ERICH WRESTLING CLAN SUFFERS DEATH OF 5TH SON—KERRY ADKISSON KILLS HIMSELF, OFFICIALS SAY

By: Jennifer Nagorka, Dan R. Barber / staff writers of the *Dallas Morning News,* Published, February 19, 1993

> Professional wrestler Kerry Von Erich ended his troubled life Thursday with a single bullet in his chest, becoming the fifth of the six brothers to die young.
>
> Tragedy has been as much a Von Erich family hallmark as athleticism, fame and the "Iron Claw" pressure-point grip. In the end, friends and officials said, Kerry struggled as much with the drug addiction and his brothers' deaths as opponents in the colorful world of professional wrestling.
>
> "He said he felt that Kerry had never worked his way through the grief of the loss of his brothers," said wrestling promoter Grey Pierson, who spoke with Kerry twice Thursday about his planned Friday night match in Dallas against a wrestler known—ironically—as the "Angel of Death."
>
> Mr. Von Erich, whose real name was Kerry Gene Adkisson, was on probation for a drug conviction and had been indicted Wednesday on

a cocaine possession charge. A warrant had been issued for his arrest. However, Mr. Pierson, president of North Star Promotions, said the 33-year-old wrestler did not seem despondent and had promised to appear as scheduled despite his legal problems. Instead, a memorial service will be held at 8 p.m. at the Sportatorium, followed by the rest of the planned matches.

"Although it was not spoken, I think he felt he was left to bear the mantle of the Von Erich wrestling dynasty. It fell on his shoulders. I think that mantle must have been a terribly heavy burden," Mr. Pierson said.

Mr. Adkisson arrived at his father's Denton County home about 1:30 p.m. Thursday and said he wanted to drive around the family property, said Denton County Sheriff's Department spokesperson Sue Morrison.

"His father got worried about him, went to look for him and found his body" about a quarter-mile north of the house, Ms. Morrison said.

Investigators found a .44-caliber Smith & Wesson handgun next to the body and a single bullet wound in his chest, Ms. Morrison said.

"This is being investigated as a possible suicide," she said. "There is no indication of foul play."

"It's a tragic story," said Steve Mr. Planamenta, a spokesman for the World Wrestling Federation, for whom Kerry Adkisson had wrestled as "The Texas Tornado." More recently, he had been a headliner for the Global Wrestling Federation as "The Modern Day Warrior."

Jack Adkisson tried to absorb the latest tragedy while surrounded by friends in the kitchen of his renovated farmhouse. He moved back to the Shady Shores area last summer as he and his wife were getting a divorce.

Looking shaken and drawn, Mr. Adkisson declined to comment about his son's death.

"I just can't say anything right now," he said. "I just do not know what I would say."

"I can remember watching Fritz as a child; I was 4 or 5 years old," said friend Renee Valadez."When you think wrestling, you think of the first family of wrestling. The Von Erich's, regardless of all the hardships, they were it."

"It's like I just talked to you yesterday," Ms. Valadez said in a soft, halting voice, referring to a conversation with a reporter 17 months ago, when Chris Adkisson took his life.

The World Wrestling Federation's Mr. Planamenta recalled Kerry Adkisson as "very religious, very family-oriented."

However, a 1986 motorcycle accident, in which he lost a foot, apparently left Mr. Adkisson addicted to prescription drugs.

"People knew he had a substance abuse problem, and certainly tried to help as much as we could," Mr. Planamenta said. "It seemed something that was very difficult for him to overcome."

Despite his apparent addiction, Mr. Adkisson had compassion for others and liked to help with charity events, Mr. Planamenta said. The World Wrestling Federation often brings children with disabilities or terminally ill children to wrestling matches.

"If Kerry knew there was a child in the building who had a disability or something, he'd want to go meet this kid," Mr. Planamenta said. "He was very good with the community."

FANS BID WRESTLER GOODBYE
3,000 Attend Tribute to Kerry Von Erich

By: Sylvia Martinez and Todd J. Gillman / staff writers for the *Dallas Morning News,* Published, February 20, 1993

An estimated 3,000 wrestling fans poured into the Sportatorium Friday night to say tearful goodbyes to Kerry Adkisson, whose death Thursday claimed a fifth member of the Von Erich wrestling family.

While many fans mourned privately, others sobbed at ringside on the night their hero had been scheduled to fight a wrestler known as the Angel of Death.

At the center of the ring, bouquets of flowers and plants sat at the base of a display that included a large color photo of the wrestler, the sequined jacket he once wore and a pair of his fringed wrestling boots.

During the ceremony, wrestlers, friends, and wrestling promoters recounted their last conversations and last visits with Mr. Adkisson. Dallas City Council member Al Lipscomb read a letter to the Adkisson family from the mayor and City Council and the Rev. James Robison asked fans to "pray now, especially for Kevin (the Adkissons' only surviving son) and let him carry on as an ambassador of life and hope."

A MOTHER'S STORY

Despite the death of five of her six sons, the matriarch of the Von Erich wrestling family finds hope in living and faith in God

By: Nancy Kruh / staff writer of the *Dallas Morning News*
Published, April 18, 1993

JEFFERSON, Texas—Doris Adkisson knows people will want to search her story. She knows they will be searching for something, anything she did wrong. She knows they will want answers so they will not make the same mistake—so their children will not die like Doris Adkisson's have.

First, Jack Jr., just 6 years old, perfect and healthy in every way. Electrocuted in a freak accident in 1959. Then David, a strong, rugged 24-year-old athlete, wrestling under the flamboyant name his dad made famous: Von Erich. Killed by an intestinal disease in 1984.

Then Mike, Chris, and Kerry Von Erich—wrestlers all and each struck down by his own hand. Three suicides in six years, three more of her babies to bury.

If you want answers, Doris Adkisson will save you the trouble of reading her story. Go, she will tell you. Do not look here. Go. Look in the book of Job.

Read in the Bible about a man who did no wrong and still lost everything. He lost his livestock, his servants, his seven sons, and three daughters. Reduced to sitting on a dung heap, scraping his open sores with a pottery shard, asking, why God, why?

Why? Because bad things happen to good people. Because bad things happen to bad people.

Because bad things happen. Only God knows why.

"The book of Job," says Ms. Adkisson, "is my book." Powerful faith.

******

Spring has arrived none too soon for Ms. Adkisson, bringing to an end a bleak winter that took away Kerry, the fifth of her sons to die. The dogwood and forsythia have burst into bloom in this quaint East Texas town that has been her home for almost a year. In her yard, a brown thrasher is building a nest, and two cardinals are noisily courting in the trees. The sky is clear, the breeze is warm, and on this day, all that Doris Adkisson wants is "my own dirt," so she can plant again. If her house did not belong to someone else—she has been renting it for the past several months—she would be outside on her knees, putting in bulbs and young plants.

It is a small yearning, smaller than anyone would expect of a mother who has lost all but one of her children. Then again, how could anyone know what to expect after something so unimaginable has happened? Just the other day, says Ms. Adkisson, who is 60, she finally heard the story that has been floating around this tiny little town; sitting at the window, alone and pining.

Ms. Adkisson laughs. Yes, she has been doing a lot of sitting at that window. "This house gets so cold," she said, "it is the only room I can keep warm." It is a cozy little breakfast nook that she has turned into a TV room, with a day bed and a small space heater.

The people who spread the story are not friends of Ms. Adkisson's and probably don't know much more than the showy careers of her ex-husband and sons and the family's very public tragedy.

"I am convinced of heaven," she says. "The more tragedy that hits, the more heavenward I look. I think that happens to everyone who is a Christian." If only that were true, says her friend of 30 years, Ann Forester. "The one thing Doris has had is the strength that has come over and over in her faith," says Ms. Forester, who is a Christian counselor in Dallas. "It is nothing mystical. It is nothing ethereal. It is very real—very practical and real. Then she acts on it. So many of us do not trust God enough to act on it."

Finding Meaning

Ms. Adkisson used to be one of those people. She remembers what it was like to be one of those "Sure, I am a Christian" Christians who show up at church for baptisms, weddings, and Easter.

Those days started back in late 1940s, when she was Doris Smith, a Dallas schoolgirl, a student at Woodrow Wilson High who "was carefree, with all those dreams…getting married, getting a job maybe," she recalls. "I wanted to start out as an airline flight attendant for the travel business. I wanted to know what the world was like."

Never a thought about motherhood, she says, and certainly not about the life she had by her 20s—bumping along two-lane blacktops, crisscrossing the county, the wife of a professional wrestler.

She had married Jack Adkisson, a football player at Southern Methodist University, when she was 17. His injuries quickly stalled his career in pro football, so he turned to the rough-and-tumble morality play of wrestling.

There have always been good guys and bad guys, and Jack Adkisson was the baddest of the bad—a fictional Nazi who called himself Fritz Von Erich. From one place to the next, he wrestled with a ferocity that fans loved to hate.

"New York, Alberta, Illinois…," Ms. Adkisson says, trying to recount the blur of the places they had lived for only a few months at a time. "St. Louis, Des Moines, Minneapolis, back to New York, Houston…"

At first, they lived in cheap motels, including one that, after several days, she realized was a brothel. Eventually, the young couple bought a trailer. Eight feet wide, thirty-seven feet long. The closest thing to a home they could afford.

It was an unusual life, but in many ways it was exactly what almost every young woman was doing back in the 1950s—being a wife, becoming a mother and, always, staying in the background. "I went right from being Mommy and Daddy's little girl," she said, "to being Fritz's wife."

She started having sons in 1952. First Jack Jr., then Kevin in '57, then David in '58. She discovered that she loved being a mom. On the other hand, maybe it was more than love. Motherhood seemed to define her. To this day, it is at the core of who she is.

"She played a lot more important role in the family than most people know," says Kevin Adkisson, now 35, her sole surviving son. "My dad was the provider, the role model. My mother…she gave us what we needed. The consideration. She loved us so much."

The first death still rivets Ms. Adkisson. Such an incomprehensible death. A little boy. An exposed power line. A chance touch. A sudden, fatal shock.

As she recounts the story, her eyes dart, focusing on the past, completely transported back to that time. Her husband is on the road. She is alone, at the hospital, and no one has the courage to tell her what has happened.

"I said to the doctor, 'is he going to be alright?' He said, 'No.' I said, 'Well, how bad is he?' He said, 'About as bad off as you can be.' Finally he said, 'He is dead'—and I passed out.

"When I woke up, I was convinced it was a horrible nightmare. It was so crazy."

She still was on unfamiliar terms with God—talking to him, but not knowing how to listen. "Right after Fritz died, I went out in the yard and said, 'God, send a sign that he is in heaven.' But I knew I should not have asked, and immediately apologized."

The boy's death made the Adkissons long to end their nomadic life, to make a stable home for their family. They returned to Texas for good. Mr. Adkisson began wrestling around Dallas and traveling alone. Ms. Adkisson had more sons to raise. Kerry in 1960, Mike in '64, and Chris in'69. Somewhere along the way, as Fritz became more famous, the line between Adkisson and Von Erich became blurred. The boys got into fights with kids who wanted to whip a Von Erich. A teacher once scolded Chris that he "had not earned the Von Erich name." The notoriety turned the boys inward, making them more close-knit, more reliant on one another.

Ms. Adkisson relishes those times together, when she and her sons would tease one another, laugh, and play. That there were good times is undeniable; the evidence is in Ms. Adkisson's face, where lines have been deeply etched by her smile and laughter.

Growing up, all the sons had a wry, off-the-wall sense of humor. They were all boisterous, adventuresome, and athletic—anything they wanted to be on a big stretch of ranch land they called home just north of Dallas.

Life was getting better, except that, Ms. Adkisson says, there was still an empty place inside her that no amount of good fortune could fill.

She prayed. She searched the scriptures. She searched her soul.

One epiphany arrived on four legs. Her name was Katie, and she was the pregnant cow that Ms. Adkisson had asked her husband to buy. A year after Katie had her calf, though, she still had not weaned her baby. Ms. Adkisson did not know that was hurting the cow until a neighbor told her.

"We had to separate them," she recalls. "I put Katie out in the pasture, and I locked up her calf in the barn. And they bawled. The little calf cried for its mother. And the mother cried for her calf. It was heartbreaking. I went out and said,

'Katie, this is not something I'm doing to hurt you. And it's not forever. It's going to be a short time.' I said, 'Katie, I wish you could understand my words, but I guess my mind is higher than yours.'

"And suddenly, it dawned on me, that's Scripture. 'For my thoughts are not your thoughts, neither are your ways my ways.' Isaiah 55. It starts at verse 8. That Scripture just came into my mind, and I had a warm feeling. That was what God was telling me about Jack Jr. He could not explain it to me, but it was not to harm me."

Though she could not have known it at the time, this revelation was to become the armor that would gird her for the tragedies yet to come.

She says she did not raise her sons to be wrestlers. She had tried to show them there were other things in the world—music lessons, even ballroom dancing. But one by one, they gravitated toward athletics. As a son would follow his father into medicine or politics, so did she see her children entering the family business. Then the family business changed.

Tragedy on tragedy. By the early 1980s, Kevin, David, and Kerry Von

Erich were attracting a whole new generation of fans to wrestling. The three brothers were the good guys, and no wrestler before them had ever had it so good. Overnight, it seemed, they were teen-age idols, regularly mobbed by fans. Thousands turned out for public appearances; hundreds of thousands watched their televised matches.

"I had no idea it was going to skyrocket." Ms. Adkisson says. "I didn't expect the boys to shoot into this star thing.

"It was like riding a shooting star. You have no idea when it will stop. But it will stop."

The first tragedy that yanked the family back to earth was David's death in 1984. While in Japan on a wrestling tour, he collapsed and died of an undetected inflammation of the intestine.

Somehow, to fans, the death made the Von Erichs more heroic. For a time, the crowds continued to gather. Then, year by year, interest in the sport waned, business squabbles grew and, for the Adkissons, tragedy piled on tragedy.

First, Mike contracted toxic shock syndrome after a routine shoulder operation in 1985. His fever spiked to 107 degrees, and doctors gave up hope. A circle of family and friends prayed—deep, gut-wrenching prayer—and Mike pulled back from the edge of death. Ms. Adkisson considers it a God-given miracle. "After the toxic shock," she says, "I'd take Mike's sweet face in my hands and say, 'Oh God, I'm glad you're alive.'"

The blessing lasted less than two years. Ravaged by the infection, depressed by his slow recovery, Mike Adkisson, at age 23, took an overdose of sleeping pills in 1987.

He left a note: "Dear Mom, you've always been wonderful. I'm in a better place, and Dave and I will be watching." Chris was next. The youngest and smallest of the sons, he had suffered from severe asthma since infancy. He desperately wanted to be like his brothers, though, and so he wrestled. He wrestled until his body inevitably failed him. In 1991, the 21-year-old man put a gun to his head.

On Feb. 4 this year, faced with a failed marriage, mounting debts and a prison sentence for a cocaine conviction, Kerry, too, shot himself. That afternoon at a Dallas restaurant, the 33-year-old wrestler had scribed on a paper tablecloth, "Tonight, I walk with my brothers."

As Ms. Adkisson talks of David's death, Mike's death, Chris' death, Kerry's death, the eyes dart, and she is back in the midst of her pain once again. "I get through what needs to be done," she says, recounting her reaction to each death. "As the pain—the sudden, wrenching pain of the loss, as it goes up and crushes my heart—I think, hold up, hold up. There are things to do. I need to find my children. I need to tell my children."

Tidal waves of despair.

After David died, she remembers bringing her four surviving sons together. "I broke the news to them as gently as I could," she says. "We all stayed together and cried."

Then she went off to grieve alone. She went to a secluded place, and she filled the quiet with a wail, a mother's wail. "I just let it out, crying to God," she says. "When your heart is breaking, it can take your breath away. The pain is so intense that you just gasp for breath."

She repeated this grim exercise—telling her children, then finding her own place to grieve—after Mike's death, after Chris' death.

After Kerry's death, "there was no one else but Kevin. There were no more children to tell."

Each death has brought a new task, a new time to deal with grief upon grief. Each has been harder to take than the last. Each has also prepared her for the next.

"In a way, it's five times worse," she says about her coping with Kerry's death. "In another way, it is comforting. I know what to expect. I know how empty my arms will feel. I know I will have that fear of forgetting his face. I know the process of grief. I know what will come next—the tidal waves of despair and helplessness and pain….Oh, God, my baby is gone.

"Then the tidal waves will be less and less. Slowly they do not come as often, and they are less painful and you are able to put them aside.

"I'm in different stages for each one. I still grieve for my 6-year-old. None of them you get over."

With the suicides, in particular, she has had to deal with the complexity of the whys. "There really aren't any words (to explain suicide)," she says. "Then again, there's no room for all the words."

She now knows that, among some people, there is a predisposition to suicide. "Somehow it is almost like a contagious disease. Somewhere in your soul, there's a little seed that says, 'Here's an alternative.' When that seed gets planted, that's the bad thing."

Just as her children were all different, so were the suicides. "In each of my children's case," she says, "there is a circumstance that pushed them past that (breaking) point."

Mike's note, she says, was not an apology. "He was convinced he was going to a better place."

Chris' suicide, she believes, was only halfhearted. "I think he was toying with an idea when the gun went off. I didn't feel like the note he left was written with conviction." Kerry's problems, she knew, were piling up far faster than expedient solutions. "Things were not going to get better, and he was too tired to laugh them off. He put off looking for options until the options began fading away."

In dealing with each suicide, she also has had to work through her feelings of guilt. "It's not that I blame myself," Ms. Adkisson says, "but I think, could I have done something differently?"

'A good mother'

In her heart, says her friend Ann Forester, Ms. Adkisson knows she was a good mother. "I talked to her probably three hours after Kerry's death," Ms. Forester recalls. "I just said, 'Doris, you are a good mother.' And she said, 'I know that.' You knew that she had bared her heart before God and come away with the sense that she'd done the best she could."

Once past the guilt, yet another question has awaited Ms. Adkisson: Why didn't any of her sons come to her for help?

In time, she says, she has come to realize that "the reasons they're hurting are the ones they can't talk to you about. They (suicide victims) actually believe they're sparing you the pain."

Or they have tunneled into their own despair so deeply that they can overlook the pain their death may cause. Ms. Adkisson says she talked to Kerry, in particular, about the pain of losing a son. "Kerry knew my feelings," she says, "but the other thing was bigger."

Reason enough, it would seem, for Ms. Adkisson to be angry, yet she will not bow to that emotion. Ms. Forester says her friend has done the hardest thing for a mother to do. She has let go of her children to live their own lives, to do, as they will—even if that means taking their own lives.

"I don't see that they took anything from me," Ms. Adkisson says. "I understand the feelings that make you do things you would not do ordinarily. I understand how they loved me, and what they did wasn't done to harm me." It's a treacherously narrow path she has maneuvered, between the guilt and the anger. But she doesn't think it's any feat. There are worse pains to endure than hers, she says. The pain of a child's murder, for instance—"to me, I can't imagine what that pain would be like, that someone jerked away that life. My sons' lives weren't stolen from them."

'I still love life'

Today, in her drafty, rented house, Doris Adkisson is at peace. Ann Forester says that is not hard to see. "If a woman is ever at a point where she's really content," Ms. Forester says, "I think Doris is, even in grief."

It is a whole new chapter for Doris Adkisson now, unfettered by a strained marriage that finally broke last year under the weight of the tragedies. To Ms. Adkisson, the end of her 42-year marriage was not so much a divorce as a declaration of independence.

She moved to Jefferson to start anew, to answer the question, "What do I want to do with my life?" She likes living alone. She also likes the fact that her son, Kevin, and his family are only a few minutes away.

She does not think twice when someone asks in passing, "How're you doing?" "I'm doing well," she says. "I'm doing well."

There are grandchildren to adore. There is a house, originally bought for Kerry, that she is going ahead and refurbishing. There is her passion for antique hunting. There are her plans to learn more about the stock market, to go back to the oil painting she once took up, to find a home of her own with her own dirt.

And yes, there is joy. There is laughter

"As much as I know the Lord, as much as I know there's a heaven, and as much as I know my kids are there, I still have the instinct to do. I still love life."

And when the pain comes, as it does with regularity, she asks God, "Can you take away any of it?...Just for a little while?"

God does, she says, every time.

Every night, as she has done for years, she recites her prayers and reads her Scripture. It may not give her answers, but it gives her understanding.

Her hope and her promise she finds in Isaiah 49: "Lift up your eyes and look around; all your sons gather and come to you. As surely as I live," declares the Lord, "you will wear them all as ornaments; you will put them on, like a bride."

Doris Adkisson knows those words were written just for her. She remembers how it feels to have her sons' arms wrapped around her. Someday she will wear them all again.

******

Kerry Von Erich won the following titles in his career:

NWA TEXAS TAG-TEAM TITLE
07/23/1979—with Bruiser Brody
05/20/1980—with Tiger Conway Jr.
08/01/1980—with Sweet Brown Sugar

NWA AMERICAN TAG-TEAM TITLE
05/04/1980—with Bruiser Brody
09/19/1980—with El Halcon
01/11/1981—with Bruiser Brody
08/10/1982—with Kevin Von Erich
06/17/1983—with Bruiser Brody
09/20/1985—with Kevin Von Erich

NWA AMERICAN HEAVYWEIGHT TITLE
12/28/1980
06/04/1980
03/08/1982
10/29/1984

NWA WORLD TAG-TEAM TITLE (TEXAS)
10/12/1981—with Terry Orndorff
12/15/1981—with Al Madrill
04/13/1982—with Al Madrill

NWA MISSOURI HEAVYWEIGHT TITLE
01/23/1983

WCCW WORLD SIX-MAN TAG-TEAM TITLE
07/04/1983—with Kevin and David Von Erich
12/02/1983—with Kevin and David Von Erich
05/06/1984—with Kevin and Mike Von Erich
09/03/1984—with Kevin and Mike Von Erich
12/31/1984—with Kevin and Mike Von Erich
09/02/1985—with Kevin Von Erich and Brian Adias
05/04/1986—with Kevin and Lance Von Erich
07/08/1988—with Kevin Von Erich and Michael Hayes

NWA WORLD HEAVYWEIGHT TITLE
05/06/1984—Kerry Von Erich defeats Ric Flair

WCWA WORLD TAG-TEAM TITLE
11/25/1987—with Kevin Von Erich
07/01/1988—with Kevin Von Erich
02/11/1989—with Kevin Von Erich
03/12/1989—with Jeff Jarrett

WCWA WORLD HEAVYWEIGHT TITLE
03/06/1988
05/08/1988
11/04/1988

TEXAS HEAVYWEIGHT TITLE
10/20/1989
01/05/1990
06/01/1990

WWF INTERCONTINENTAL HEAVYWEIGHT TITLE
08/27/1990

WWWA HEAVYWEIGHT TITLE
10/22/1992

USWF HEAVYWEIGHT TITLE
12/28/1992

CHAPTER 12

After Kerry's funeral I just went home and locked myself in the house on my 150-acre Lake Dallas ranch, refusing to see or talk to anyone until I had time to sort out all the things that had happen to me and my family over the past several years. I tried to make some sense of how my three sons could have taken their own lives. Why had I not seen this coming? Were Doris and I to blame for not forcing ourselves into their lives and making them sit down and talk to us and tell me and their mother what was on their minds? For months, questions poured into my head that I could not seem to find answers to.

One night, I woke up from a dream about Kerry. In the dream I could see Kerry getting into the jeep and driving past me, not even looking in my direction. Then, I was standing beside my house and kept hearing over and over what Kerry's girlfriend had told me that evening, sitting in the swing behind the house just before Kerry had shot himself through the heart. I woke up that morning in a hard sweat, remembering that she told me that Kerry and Kevin had a big argument over the phone, and I began to wonder why Kevin had not said anything to me about that night. Why had I forgotten about what Kerry's girlfriend had told me that day? Why did Kevin not tell me about that phone call from Kerry? Later that day, I phoned Kevin in Jefferson, Texas, where he and his family were living at the time. I told him that when he had some spare time I wanted him to come and see me, and we could spend the day together and have lunch.

Kevin drove down the next day and he and I went out to lunch. After returning to the house, the two of us sat down at the kitchen table for some small talk about the grandkids and what was going on in his life. About thirty minutes into our conversation, I got around to Kerry and I repeated what Kerry's girlfriend had told me that evening. Kevin turned pale as a ghost as he sat there, stunned at what I had just relayed to him. A few minutes passed, and Kevin looked up at me and said that he had wanted to talk to me over the past couple of months about Kerry, but could not find the words.

"Dad," Kevin said, "Kerry did phone me that night, and we did get into an argument. It was around two o'clock in the morning and I was in bed asleep.

He sounded as if he was drunk or stoned because I could not understand some of the things he was saying; he was talking out of his head. He told me that his trial was coming up in the next few weeks and he knew that the judge was going to send him to prison. Kerry said that he felt that he could not go to jail, that he was thinking about killing himself. Dad, you know how after Kerry's motorcycle accident he told us that if he would not be able to wrestle again, that he might as well blow his head off? I did not take him seriously because he had told me several times that he felt his life was over. I tried to calm him down but he would keep arguing with me; I told him that the family would not let that happen to him. After about half an hour of trying to make some sense out of the things he was saying, I got mad and told him that if that is what he really wanted to do, then he needed to go ahead and do it and stop telling me every time he called. I never thought that he was really going to go through with it, Dad."

After hearing these words from my oldest son, a sick feeling trickled through my entire body. "My God, Kevin! Kerry called you for help. Why did you tell him that?" I screamed. "Why didn't you call your mother or me and let us know that he was thinking about taking his own life? That was your brother you told to go ahead and kill himself, all because you were asleep and could not be bothered. If anyone talks about taking their own life, you need to listen to them and try to help them the best way you can—is that not what the doctors told us when Mike was having all his problems? You were there that day the doctors told us that, Kevin, remember? I cannot believe that you would keep this from me and not tell me about that phone call! Because of you, Kerry is dead."

Kevin left that day without saying much of anything else. I just sat there, still trying to sort things out in my mind. I could not help but think that if Kevin had handled things differently, Kerry might still be alive. At this point I started thinking back to when I found Kerry on the ground, still clutching the .44 revolver in his hand, and the thoughts that were running through my head of using it on myself. After all, what did I have to live for now? All my children but one were dead, my wife had left me, I could hardly walk, and could not hear a thing without my hearing aids, and I honestly felt I was a fool for hanging around any longer. I would find myself thinking these kinds of thoughts for a long time, until one day I realized that my three sons had more than likely thought the same types of things before they killed themselves. I could not take my own life because I felt it was wrong; it was taking the easy way out and avoiding responsibility for my and my family's actions.

It took me several weeks of blaming Kevin for Kerry's death before I realized that Kevin was the only son I had left and I needed to try to understand that he did not know that Kerry would do such a thing. I knew that Kevin loved his brothers and would have done anything in order to help them. I felt deep down inside my heart that Kevin had made a big mistake and it was tearing him up inside, and I was just making matters worse by not telling him that I loved him and did not blame him for what had happened.

Months later, I still blamed Kevin in the back of my mind for Kerry's death. However, after much thought, I finally called Kevin and apologized by saying that none of us could have known what the outcome of Kerry's life could have been, and that I was just upset because he did not call me that night and tell me about what was on Kerry's mind.

Kevin had to settle with the IRS shortly after Kerry's death, which left him broke. He was living in a house in Jefferson that belonged to his mother. After I apologized to Kevin that morning for not seeing his side of things, I told him that he could have a house built on the 150 acres if he wanted to move to Lake Dallas and live down the road from me and I would pay for it. He agreed.

Kevin is my second oldest son and I love him very much, but he was always closest to his mother. We have not really seen eye to eye for quite a few years. I'm sure you noticed, Ron, on that day you volunteered to stay and take care of me, that Kevin never offered the same, and he only lives three hundred yards from me. I hate to say this, but Kevin has always felt that I cheated him and his brothers out of money from all the Texas Stadium matches back when they were kids and just getting started in the business. One day before Kerry shot himself and the two of them were having all kinds of financial problems, they came to me and asked for money to keep the Sportatorium running. This was when Kevin first brought all this up to me, saying that he knew how much money the promotion took in the night of the Parade of Champions and other Texas Stadium matches, and that he and his brothers did not get their fair share. This had really made me mad to the point that I told him that just because he and his brothers had blown all their money on parties and drugs and I had invested mine in real estate and the stock market and had more than tripled it, he should not be thinking some of it belonged to him. I told him that of the millions of dollars that were taken in from those matches, he did not understand how much it took to put on those shows. All he had to do was go over all the receipts that I still kept in my desk drawer and he could have seen for himself. He and his brothers got the share that all of us had agreed on. Kerry had just stood there all this time not saying a word; when I asked him what he thought, he said, "Gee, Dad, I don't think you cheated us; that's just what Kevin said." Kevin stormed out of the house, telling Kerry that he had always been my favorite son and would agree with anything I said.

After I turned the business over to Kevin and Kerry I had high hopes that it would make both those boys develop a good business sense. I was wrong. The two of them had so many problems keeping good business records. That was what caused their IRS problems. A few months before Kevin and Kerry filed for bankruptcy and showed up at the house that morning asking for money, I got a call from a Dallas police detective who said they were getting reports of drugs being sold at the Sportatorium. This had concerned me to no end. It had not been that long ago that one of the wrestlers who worked for WCCW was shot dead in the Sportatorium parking lot. I will not mention any names, but he had been linked to organized crime and the sale of cocaine. So in a way, deep down inside, I was glad that Kevin and Kerry were being forced into filing for bankruptcy and giving the business up.

I never told the two boys that the police were watching the Sportatorium. I really just wanted them out of the business altogether. I was very afraid that somehow the police were going to find some way to link Kevin and Kerry to those drugs, so I refused to bail out the Sportatorium and told the two boys that I could not help them and that they would be better off to close the doors and find something else to do with their lives.

After thinking back on what I told Kevin and Kerry that day, I feel it was the wrong thing to tell them. I guess in the back of Kerry's mind the Sportatorium was all he had left, and I have always felt that I took that away from him. Maybe you can see how I have beat myself up all these years wondering if things could have been different if I had just done things another way. Part of me has blamed myself all these years for taking the Sportatorium away from Kevin and Kerry. If Kerry had had the Sportatorium to fall back on, he might still be alive.

CHAPTER 13

This chapter belongs to Kevin Ross Adkisson, the second-oldest of the six brothers and the last of the wrestling Von Erich boys. Kevin grew up taking care of his brothers and he was always there for them. He was the one who learned from his father and passed his knowledge down to his younger brothers.

Kevin has long since retired from pro wrestling and lives a quiet life with his wife, Pam, and their four children—Christen, Jill, Ross, and Marshal—on the Von Erich ranch on Lake Dallas in Denton County, Texas, that his father loved so much. Kevin and I were friends for quite a few years, and in that time he told me many stories about himself and his family. Now I will try to share some of those stories with all the Von Erich fans out there.

Kevin's family comes before everything else in his life and always has. He is a good husband and a very dedicated father who is always playing with his children. Kevin takes the time to talk to his children and teach them things just as his dad took the time to teach him.

Naturally, Kevin cannot help wondering why he is the only Von Erich brother still alive. On several occasions, Kevin has said to me that the only difference he could find between himself and his brothers was that he had a wife and family that he loved more than wrestling. David, Kerry, Mike, and Chris had always been infatuated with all the bright lights and lifestyle that came from being a pro wrestling star.

"Pam and I got married a few years after I started my wrestling career," Kevin explained. "I had already wrestled around the world and was ready to settle down and raise a family. After I got married, Dave and Kerry were still traveling all over the world from show to show. I would try to wrestle in Texas and the United States so I could come home as much as possible, only venturing out of the States when I had to defend a title or tag with David and Kerry."

Kevin Ross Adkisson was born May 15, 1955, in Belleville, Illinois. He made his first pro wrestling debut against Paul Parsman (Buddy Rose) on August 8, 1976, in Fort Worth, Texas, winning his opening match in just under five minutes.

Kevin and I started to become friends after that night in late 1993, when he came to my house to meet me that first time. I had been very careful not to mention his brothers, knowing that Kerry had committed suicide just eight months earlier.

A couple of weeks after that first meeting, Kevin called me one day and asked if I would like to go out and eat sushi and drink a little sake. I had traveled to many parts of Japan while in the Marine Corps and Kevin and I had talked a lot about Japan and some of the places we had visited there. As it turned out, we both loved Japanese cuisine—so much so that our meals would run about $150 for the two of us, plus tip. Our favorite Japanese restaurant was Ichijo Japanese Cuisine, located on Beltline Road in Irving. The restaurant's owner and Master Chef, Akiko Mimura, told us that she had never seen two men eat so much sushi and enjoy it as much as the two of us. Akiko would tell Kevin and me how she remembered when Fritz first came to Japan, and all the commotion that was caused when Fritz defeated the Giant Baba.

During that first dinner at the Japanese restaurant, Kevin started talking about his brothers and all the great times that he, Dave, and Kerry had shared growing up. Kevin told me to feel free to ask any questions I might have about him and his brothers, saying it did not bother him to discuss the subject.

Kevin told me that he, Dave, and Kerry were all just a few years apart and were as close as three brothers could possibly be. "The three of us got along so well together; we had a mutual love and respect for one another that went beyond just being brothers."

Here is the story of Kevin and his brothers, in Kevin's own words:

When the three of us were growing up together, we were really into natural things. When our family bought the 150 acres on Lake Dallas, we had everything that boys could want growing up. We would spend our time in the woods as much as possible, hunting and fishing and catching any wild animals we could find. The three of us would swim anywhere there was water—in ponds, creeks, lakes—and anywhere we could get wet.

One summer, Dave, who was around thirteen years old at the time, got to spend a couple of weeks with a friend whose father took them scuba diving in one of the local lakes. Dave said he could hardly wait to get back home to tell Kerry and me of the new world he had discovered. For the rest of the summer, scuba diving was all Dave could talk about. His enthusiasm was infectious, and it was not long before he had Kerry and me both dreaming of the upcoming summer. We picked up some dive magazines and made plans to go scuba diving the following summer. We planned for months, and when Christmas came around that year, Mom and Dad got a rather large list of all the things that Dave and I would need for our upcoming diving trip. That summer, Dave taught me how to scuba dive; Mom and Dad felt that Kerry was too young at the time, so the summer after that, Dave and I taught Kerry. Later, as we grew up and began to wrestle and travel on our own, we would go diving together all over the world.

One of the best memories I have about Dave and me was the time that we discovered diving in Hawaii. I had lived in Hawaii for a while one summer and drove a taxicab around the island before Pam and I got married, and really learned to love the islands. Dave and I had both been wrestling in Japan at the time and I had not been married very long. We were due to go on a wrestling tour of the Middle East and had a few weeks to kill before we had to be there, so I called my wife Pam and told her to meet Dave and me in Hawaii. Kerry was still in college at the time and had not yet started his wrestling career.

Dave and I got to Hawaii a few days before Pam arrived and we had more fun than I think I have ever had before. We decided to try scuba diving at night, and it was like nothing we had ever experienced before. There were so many more fish than during the day. We would dive at night at a local reef, catch lobsters by the bagful, and spear many different types of fish. Then we would eat what we wanted and give the rest to the kitchen at the motel where we were staying. The chef really loved us there and would fix us different dishes from all over the world. When we checked out three weeks later, they sure hated to see us leave.

I think that I was closer to Dave than my other brothers. We were always doing everything together when we were kids before Kerry was old enough to hang around with us. Dave and I were always trying to see which one of us could catch the biggest snake or the most spiders. Things that other kids thought were weird, Dave and I thought were cool, and I guess we passed that on to Kerry because I think he grew up to be weirder than Dave and I both.

I remember one year when Dave and I were very young and Dad let us go quail hunting with him. Dad had invited a few big shots to come hunting with us and Dave and I agreed to clean all the quail they shot that day. As with most things, Dave and I would have to make a contest out of it, and it was not long before we were neck and neck in this quail-cleaning contest. After someone shot a quail, Dave and I would not even wait for the dogs to get all the way back to us with the bird before we would take off running and meet the dog about halfway back, grab the quail from the dog's mouth, and start running back, cleaning the quail as we ran. I do not think we ever established a winner at that contest. I would win sometimes, and Dave would win sometimes, but one thing was for sure—the two of us could clean more quail faster than anyone else around.

When Pam showed up in Hawaii, Dave and I got a big surprise. Our brother Mike had come along with her. He was about thirteen or fourteen at the time, and this was his first big trip away from Mom and Dad. Dave and I had trouble believing that Mom and Dad had given him permission to come with Pam. We taught Mike how to scuba dive on that trip, and together we all had the best times exploring the islands and doing all the crazy things brothers do.

Mike was such a great person and loving brother. He had a wonderful personality and got along with everyone really well. He was always doing anything he could to help Dave, Kerry, and me. When Mike came into wrestling to take Dave's place, Kerry and I thought he was a natural. Everyone was saying Mike's wrestling style was just like David's. Everyone also thought that Mike looked a lot like Dave, so he fit in well tagging with Kerry and me. The whole family was so proud of Mike and all the fans were crazy about him, especially the girls.

Mike would have become a better wrestler than all of us, had it not been for the shoulder surgery and the toxic shock syndrome. I will never forget how bad Mike got after surgery. We finally got to go in and see him one at a time after the doctors had removed him from the critical list, and he looked awful. He had gone into the hospital for what we all thought was going to be a routine shoulder surgery, and two days later he looked almost dead. Mike had been in the best shape of his life, just winning the NWA American Heavyweight belt. I really had a hard time dealing with everything that had happened to Mike so quickly.

We were all very happy when Mike came home from the hospital, but the months that would pass would show our whole family that Mike was still very sick. I do not think he ever truly got better after getting out of the hospital. Mike had never given any sign at all that he was thinking about suicide.

His wrestling career was going great. There was just no reason for Mike to do something like that and it really did catch us all by surprise. I never looked at Mike's death as suicide because the toxic shock had caused his fever to go so high that I believe Mike was never the same person after he was released from the hospital. I just do not think that he was aware of his actions.

I always wished that Chris and I could have gone off on our own and gotten to know each other much better than we did. I was so much older than Chris that he and I never had the fun that the other brothers and I did. I was married and had a daughter who was just a few years younger than Chris was, so I always thought he looked at me more like an adult than a brother.

I loved all my brothers and wish I could have done something to help them through the problems that caused them to take their own lives, but not one of them ever gave me a clue that they were thinking about suicide. Kerry used to joke around about shooting himself after he had the motorcycle wreck and was having problems with the IRS, but I never thought he would actually do it. He was always a big practical joker and many times I would have trouble telling if Kerry was joking or if he was serious.

Kerry would call me on the phone sometimes, two or three times a month, no matter where he was at the time; he would always tell me that things were going very well for him. But Mom and Dad were worried about Kerry and they would ask me if I knew anything about his life, if he was still taking pain pills or drugs, and how he was doing mentally after the loss of his foot. However, I did not know anything. For the last few years or so of Kerry's life, he was traveling around the world wrestling for the WWF and other promoters, so it was hard to keep track of him. I had tagged with Kerry on several occasions while he was with the WWF, but I was still doing well in Texas and was at home with my family on weekends.

I loved all my brothers and have great memories of each one of them. Not many days go by that I do not think of one or all of them in some way or another. There are times when I walk around the 150-acre property where we all grew up together and remember a time long ago, a time when David, Kerry, and I were all over the land, playing games, running and laughing, with no cares or worries. Then Mom or Dad would scream at us from the house to come eat supper or to get inside and do our homework, always talking about how us boys were all going to drive them to the nuthouse someday. So many good memories, so many good times.

Before Fritz passed away, a college student from North Texas State University, Rusty Baker, approached Kevin, saying he wanted to do a documentary about Kevin and his family for a school project. Kevin and Fritz both agreed, so for more than a year, Rusty shot footage at the Von Erich ranch on Lake Dallas, and after several interviews came out with a fifty-five-minute video in 1999 entitled *Faded Glory*. The video won first place at the Fort Worth Film Festival; it was very well done and well worth watching.

I thought I would include the most recent interview with Kevin, taken by the *Dallas Morning News* almost two years after Fritz's death.

******

News articles were taken from the *Dallas Morning News* archives: all articles are printed as they appeared.

SURVIVING VON ERICH LEADS TRANQUIL LIFESTYLE

By: Cody Monk—The *Dallas Morning News*
Published, September 10, 1999

Kevin Adkisson spent Labor Day doing nothing. The 42-year-old Lake Dallas native sat on his Shady Shores ranch near Denton and watched his cattle graze on the expansive pasture behind his house.

"I love these cattle," said Adkisson, better known as wrestler Kevin Von Erich. "It's kind of funny. When I first got them, I did it just to have something. Now I really enjoy them."

The cattle give Von Erich the tranquil lifestyle he has longed for since he retired from the ring four years ago. Days like Monday are what he enjoys most. Not so much because he has time to keep a close eye on his herd, but because he has the chance to relax and enjoy things he never knew existed.

"I enjoy the peace the most," Adkisson said. "I'm enjoying the life I missed out on earlier in my life. I remember most Labor Days we would be putting on three shows. It used to be easy because all of us were around. Then David died and then it was just me running the shows. That's when it got hard."

Most of Adkisson's life has been hard. The oldest of five brothers, he is the only living member of a family who created a tradition like no other in the wrestling business.

The tradition started with patriarch Fritz Von Erich, who became one of the most dominating promoters in the country. He ran shows out of Dallas' Sportatorium and in Fort Worth. He developed some of the best-known wrestlers of the '60s, '70s and '80s. He also took his wrestlers all over the world, which put him several steps ahead of other promoters of the time.

Fritz's best wrestlers lived under his own roof. Sons David, Kerry, Mike, Chris, and Kevin all followed Fritz into the business. Tragedy though, seemed to follow the family.

In 1984, David died of an infection while wrestling in Japan.

Three years later, Mike died of a tranquilizer overdose. Chris died in 1991, Kerry committed suicide in 1994 and Fritz died in 1997.

Somehow, Adkisson was able to move on. "Someone asked Woody Allen one time if he would like to achieve immortality through his business," Adkisson said, "He said, 'I want to achieve immortality by not dying.' I guess that's what I've done."

Adkisson spends most days tending to his cattle and taking care of two sons and two daughters, who range in age from six to eighteen. He often handles the daily commute between the ranch and school in Dallas. He also works on the Von Erich web site. "I like the site," he said. "I get on there every now and then and get into the chat, but I just can't make my words come through on the computer like I want. That's a gift I don't have."

Adkisson also finds time to watch wrestling on television. Even though the current WWF and WCW are somewhat removed from the tradition of the Von Erichs, Kevin and his brothers are credited with changing the business from a slow-paced athletic event to the show fans now see.

"My brothers and I didn't like the old-man style," Adkisson said. "We didn't like to sit in the middle of the ring and exchange holds. We liked it fast-paced. We liked the up-tempo style. And we went all out. Some of the best times I remember are those times when they would just give us leather straps and we'd go beat the hell out of each other."

Adkisson also enjoys watching wrestlers he helped develop, some of whom are carrying the industry. "I enjoy watching (Stone Cold) Steve Austin," said Adkisson, who, like Austin, attended the University of North Texas on a football scholarship. "I remember when he started at Chris (Adams') school. He was always so charismatic. He would go anywhere to wrestle a show. I would come in and help Chris and some of his top students. I remember wrestling Steve when he was just a student. Of course, he looked a lot different than he does now."

Adkisson also worked with a 6-9, 320-pounder his father had found working as a bouncer in Arlington. "We called him 'The Punisher,'" said Adkisson, referring to Mark Callaway, now the WWF's The Undertaker. "He wouldn't say anything. I'd wrestle him and he wouldn't ever look at me. He never made eye contact. He was a big star, but he would just stand there and look at your knees or boots."

In Kevin's twenty-year career, he won the following titles:

NWA TEXAS TAG-TEAM TITLE
04/07/1978—with David Von Erich
09/04/1978—with David Von Erich

NWA AMERICAN TAG-TEAM TITLE
10/16/1978—with David Von Erich
08/21/1982—with Kerry Von Erich
09/20/1985—with Kerry Von Erich

NWA AMERICAN HEAVYWEIGHT TITLE
12/25/1978
01/12/1980
04/28/1980
09/05/1982
03/04/1983

NWA MISSOURI HEAVYWEIGHT TITLE
11/23/1979

NWA WORLD TAG-TEAM TITLE (TEXAS)
02/09/1981—with David Von Erich

ALL-ASIAN TAG-TEAM TITLE
05/23/1981—with David Von Erich

ALL-ASIAN TAG-TEAM TITLE (DALLAS)
02/11/1982—with David Von Erich

WCCW WORLD SIX-MAN TAG-TEAM TITLE
07/04/1983—with David and Kerry Von Erich
12/02/1983—with David and Kerry Von Erich
05/06/1984—with Fritz and Mike Von Erich
09/03/1984—with Kerry and Mike Von Erich
12/31/1984—with Kerry and Mike Von Erich
09/02/1985—with Kerry Von Erich and Brian Adias
05/04/1986—with Kerry and Lance Von Erich
07/08/1988—with Kerry Von Erich and Michael Hayes

WCWA WORLD HEAVYWEIGHT TITLE

10/12/1986

WCWA WORLD TAG-TEAM TITLE

11/25/1987—with Kerry Von Erich
07/01/1988—with Kerry Von Erich
03/22/1989—with Kerry Von Erich

TEXAS HEAVYWEIGHT TITLE

07/04/1988

TWF TEXAS HEAVYWEIGHT TITLE

02/03/1991

WCCW TAG-TEAM TITLE

03/06/1993—with Chris Adams

CHAPTER 14

After Kerry died, Doris and I sold our retirement dream house near Edom, Texas, and went our separate ways. I moved into the small frame house that has been on the Lake Dallas property for years. Doris told me she did not know where she was going or what she was going to do, but that she would keep in touch with me.

Just across the highway and woods in front of this small house on Shady Shores is where we built the first house that Doris designed by drawing her sketches on butcher paper.

Officials in Lake Dallas named the street in front of that house "Fritz Lane." They wanted to name it "Iron Claw Lane," but Doris threw a fit and announced that she absolutely would not live any place called Iron Claw Lane. It took some doing and a lot of talking to people, but I finally got them to agree to Fritz Lane. We donated that house and the property it sat on to the church when we built our retirement home near Edom, leaving me with the 150-acre Lake Dallas property that I live on now. When I am dead and gone, it will all belong to Kevin and his family. I can only hope that Kevin will hold on to it and pass it on to his children.

I sit here day after day and wonder what went so wrong in my life. Why is it that my wife and I are not sitting in a rocker on our front porch in Edom, enjoying a whole bunch of grandchildren? Life can sure be cruel.

Some days I think of all the good times in my life when the boys were young and the family was together and we all had so much fun. Those are my best days. Then there are the days when all I can think about are the unexpected deaths of five of my sons. I cannot stop thinking about that strange voice on the other end of the phone, telling me one of my sons has been found dead. I have spent countless hours sitting around this house thinking about Jack Jr., David, Mike, Chris, and Kerry, and wondering what life would have been like for them if things had been just a little different.

Mostly, I blame myself, just as I think most parents would if something like this happened in their family. If only I had been able to talk to those boys before they killed themselves. I still feel after all these years that if Kevin had called me that night Kerry told him he was going to take his life, that I could have stepped in and stopped it. Kerry and I had always been so close. If only those boys had come to me or their mother with their problems before doing something so foolish. If only Doris and I could have worked things out and stayed together. If only this, if only that.

Outliving your children has to be the hardest thing in this world for any parent to have to go through. For the rest of your life you will not be able to get that child out of your mind; every day you will think about them in one way or another and how much you miss having them around.

No matter what I try to do during the day, no matter how hard I try to think about something else, my thoughts always go back to my boys and why all of this stuff had to happen to my family. Then there is always the countless number of times every week that I relive that moment when I found out one of my boys was dead. If there is such a place as hell, I think that I have already been there in my mind over the past several years.

Doris, bless her heart, was the perfect wife and mother. She could not have done more to help those boys. That woman tried so hard to make a good home for all of us. She was always there to help them and me in any way she could. So many times she was the one to hold the family together while I was on the road or overseas, and she did such a great job. When she and I got a divorce, I knew that it was not because we had quit loving one another as much as it was that so many things happened in the family so fast. She had been through so much, losing all but one of her sons, that I think she just had to get away by herself and handle things in her own way.

When I die, I will love that woman just as much as I did that night we were married before the justice of the peace in Denton, Texas.

As I mentioned to you before, when Kerry died, my belief in God stopped. I began to feel strange in church, so I quit going. I guess that I have felt for years now that when you die, it's all over. Now that the doctors have given me less than six months to live, I find myself wondering what I will face after this life. I am not sure what I believe in now. I really would like to believe that there is a God and a Heaven where we all go when we leave this world, but I am just not sure that I can. The thought of me dying and giving up this beat-up, worn-out body and seeing Jack Jr., David, Kerry, Mike, and Chris again gives me hope, but I have so many doubts about everything nowadays, including myself.

I have read and heard so many rumors about how I forced my boys into becoming wrestlers, how I did this or did that to my sons. Some reporters and other people in this world do not care how much pain they cause as long as they can get their story. Unfortunately, I could not trust many journalists to tell the truth. They would have to add this or add that in order to get people to read something into a story that just was not there. That's the biggest reason I turned down so many interviews when one son after another died. I knew that many of my best fans and all the people who had followed my boys and me for years wanted to know the truth. It makes me mad as hell to think back on the stories that were spread after my second son, David, died in Japan. There were stories that he was on drugs, stories that the Japanese mob had him killed because he had a gambling debt, stupid stories. I do not care what people might have heard or read somewhere, the truth is that David died from enteritis, which is an inflammation of the intestinal tract.

One day I read in a wrestling magazine that there was a rumor going around that the reason Kerry lost his right foot after the doctors reattached it was because I made him start working out before his foot was totally healed. The article went on to say that the reason that I made Kerry work out before his foot was healed was that the Sportatorium was starting to lose money because David and Mike were gone. Why would someone be as inconsiderate and cruel as to start such an unfounded rumor? I will not get into which publications or the dumbasses who wrote these types of article, but I have read them with my own eyes. And this, Ron, is where you come in. I am not sure why you want to spend your time taking care of a dying old man like myself, but I thank God that you are around. You have been so much help and comfort to me over these past few months, I really don't know how I can repay you. But I really need to ask one more favor of you before I go, and that is for you to write that book about myself and my family and try to put some of these unfounded rumors to rest once and for all. I know that I'm asking a lot from you, but you are the one person who I trust to tell the story just as I told it to you. And I can tell you right now that I am pretty sure that I will be proud of what you put down on paper.

I want everyone to know that I have always been very proud of who I am. I am proud of my wrestling career and what I accomplished in my life. I like to think that I and a few other old-timers did a little something to make wrestling what it has become today. I tried very hard and refused to give up, even when it seemed like I had no other choice. Sometimes it would seem like one injury after another would keep me from fulfilling my dream of becoming the best damn pro wrestler of my day, but I tried as hard as I could and refused to quit trying.

Wrestling gets in your blood. It is almost like an addiction to see all the fans gather in one city or another under one roof, waiting in line and paying their hard-earned money to see you wrestle in the main event that night.

There's nothing like the feeling you get when they put that championship belt around your waist and raise your hand high in the air for all to see, and you hear all the fans screaming out your name in the background. Nothing in this world can compare to that. Nothing!

But sometimes I can't help but to wonder what my life would have been like if one of those injuries had kept me out of that ring. What would I have done if my career had been cut short? Could I have lived with the fact that I would no longer be able to climb in that ring and do what I love most in my life? I wonder sometimes what I might have done if I had been brought up in a wrestling family as my boys were, and I had to face the same problems that caused the three of them to take their own lives. I do not know the answer to that question.

I never forced any of my sons into becoming wrestlers. As young boys they were always asking to go with me to the Sportatorium whenever I was there wrestling. They were young boys who were proud of their father and the way he made a living. They would tell everyone that when they grew up, they wanted to be professional wrestlers, just like their old man.

One article that came out almost a year after Kerry died claimed that a "reliable source" said I beat my boys and forced them to work out when they were very young so they would later become unbeatable pro wrestlers, and I could build my wrestling empire. Another said that I would not allow Mike to go to college, that I had made him give up his dream when David died so he could take his place in the ring and I could maintain my hold on my wrestling empire. Give me a break. Why would people start such stupid and unfounded rumors?

I never wanted my sons to get into the wrestling business, but when you think about it, pro wrestling was all those boys ever knew After I came to Texas and started gaining many fans throughout the state, the boys reached that age where I started taking them to the matches with me. They were around my fans, and the first thing those fans would ask the boys was, "Are you going to be a wrestler like your dad?" It was programmed in those boys at an early age. I think that just about all of our friends and most everyone the boys ran into would ask them that same question.

The only one of the boys that I ever felt was pushed into wrestling was maybe Mike. I think Mike was under a lot of pressure from friends and fans alike, because he and David favored each other so much and everyone really did expect Mike to take David's place in the ring.

At one time in Texas when Kevin, David, and Kerry were the World Six-Man Tag-Team champs, the phrase "Von Erich brothers" was all you heard around here. They were doing big commercials for Pizza Inn and other large Texas businesses. The younger generation was just getting into pro wrestling and after David died, I think that generation pushed Mike into wrestling and never gave him a chance to say no!

I loved my sons. Maybe I gave them too much when they were growing up, I do not know. When I was young and growing up in East Texas, my family was poor, as were most families during the Great Depression. There were no shopping malls or movies to go to, not even a television to watch, and most families could not even afford a radio.

Anytime the neighbors would come over or we got to go into town, all the kids would play games like baseball or football, or they would just try to see who could throw a rock the farthest, stuff like that. I loved playing all sports, and I loved competition. My family could never afford gym equipment, so I learned to make the best out of what I had.

We could not afford a football or a baseball to throw around, and there were very few kids around who owned one. So what did we do? Granddaddy Ross and I made a football out of a bunch of rags that we tied together with string, and we played baseball with an old broomstick and rocks.

Things were very hard during the Depression. Maybe that's why I gave my sons so much. I did not want those boys to grow up doing without as I did. I wanted them to play football with a football, and not with a bunch of rags tied together. Isn't that what most good parents want for their children? To give them more than what they had when they were growing up.

******

One night, after Fritz and I were on our third glass of Scotch, he asked if he had ever told me about the Von Erich curse. I had heard Kevin say a few times that he thought his family was cursed, and I remembered that Kevin's mother had even said something about a Von Erich curse a couple of times in Vicksburg, but I had not given it much thought. In fact, I always thought that Kevin talked about the curse because of the many deaths in his immediate family, or that he was just making something up.

"No," I told Fritz. "I do not think you ever mentioned that." Before Fritz started telling me the story about his grandmother, whose maiden name was Von Erich, he told me that he had never really told his family, or anyone else for that matter, the whole story about the Von Erich curse. "I may have mentioned a few times that the Von Erich name seems cursed, but I would never talk about it much because I did not want my family thinking about those kinds of things," Fritz said. "I have always felt very awkward about believing what I am about to share with you, but after many years of thinking back on my life, I have to seriously wonder if curses do exist.

"My grandmother's family came to the United States from Germany several years before World War I. While I was growing up, I would hear Granddaddy Ross and my father talk about Grandma's curse. My grandmother would always be losing something, or hurting herself in some way or another, and Granddaddy Ross would always say things like, 'It's that damn curse,' and, 'Of all the women in this world I had to fall in love with, it had to be the one woman whose family is cursed.' He would always laugh after saying it, so I always thought he was making a joke. I was so young at the time that I never paid much attention to what they were saying. I guess I thought he was just making fun of my grandmother. But years later after the loss of Jack Jr., I started remembering some of the things my grandfather had said when I was growing up.

"A few years after Jack Jr.'s funeral, we were back in Texas visiting my parents, and I asked my father about the Von Erich curse one day when we were out fishing together. My father told me that my grandmother came from a very large family and that many members of the family were killed while leaving Germany. 'After your grandmother's family got to the United States, shortly before she was born, more members of her family lost their lives due to an outbreak of some type of virus. Others starved to death in the slums of New York City before the turn of the century. When your Grandma was born, she was in poor health and barely survived. Her grandmother's mother and father were the ones who told all the children that there was a longtime curse on the Von Erich name. If I remember right, it came about by something that had happened in your grandmother's family back in Germany many years before your grandmother was even born,' my father told me. 'I do not even remember just exactly what had happened that caused them to tell their children this, but I think it had something to do with a family member who was left behind in Germany and was not allowed to come to America with the rest of the family. That about all I can remember.'

"My father went on to say that my grandmother really did believe in the curse, even though my grandfather was a little more skeptical. 'My dad did not like my mother talking about curses, so it only came up when something bad would happened in the family and they needed something to blame their misfortune on,' my dad said.

"'I had never paid much attention to her when I was growing up, and I do not even remember her talking about it that much as a boy,' my father continued. 'But now that I think about it, after we came back from your grandfather's funeral in Jewett, she made a comment that the Von Erich curse was to blame for his death and she was surprised that he had lasted as long as he did. However, she had taken your grandfather's death hard and was old and in poor health herself.'

"Then my father asked me why I was so interested in this ancient family curse. I thought for a moment and chose my words carefully. 'Dad,' I said, 'do you think that it is possible that the name Von Erich could be cursed like Grandma said?' I remember that my father looked at me somewhat funny, then after a long pause he said, 'Now, Jack, you're starting to sound like your grandmother. If you are trying to blame your bad luck and misfortune with what happened to Jack Jr. based on something that you heard back when you were young, son, forget it; there is no such thing as a curse on a name or family, and you of all people should know better that that.'

"After saying that, he immediately changed the subject and the topic of the Von Erich Curse was never mentioned again.

"I did not think much about it myself," Fritz said, "until my other sons started to die, one by one after taking that name 'Von Erich.' I have always looked to the Lord for answers in my life, but after Kerry's death and after Doris leaving me like she did, I started to think about that curse more and more. I am sure that my fans out there reading this right now think I must have lost my mind, but after you lose one family member after the other, you do what you can to try to make some kind of sense of things.

"I would never come right out and say that I believe I have been living all these years with a curse hanging over my head, but I will say that some strange things have happened to me ever since I started using the Von Erich name. I try not to let my mind dwell on such things, but after losing five of my six sons—and all but one used the name 'Von Erich' more than they did 'Adkisson'—I cannot help but wonder if there might be some truth to the story of that old curse.

"A few years ago, after Mike passed away, I even tried to trace the Von Erich family tree, but I could only trace my grandmother's family back about fifty years before World War I over in Germany before the trail died out. Maybe I am just using this curse thing as an excuse, because after Kerry killed himself I decided that I did not believe that there was a God. But still, after looking back on my life, it seems to me that strange things sure seemed to follow me around."

After Fritz had gone to bed that night, I went outside and sat on the swing that was under a large oak tree in Fritz's back yard. I thought about what Fritz had said that night and began to wonder if maybe there could be such a thing as a curse.

Fritz and his family sure had been through a lot for a family that was so close. I started to remember back when I was growing up and would read news articles and wrestling magazines about Fritz and his family; the articles would never just be about Fritz, but rather about Fritz and his family. I had always thought that the Von Erichs were the perfect family because they were always doing things together and seemed to be so happy. I would see pictures in the Dallas morning newspapers of Fritz and his boys hunting or fishing together. I would hardly ever see an interview on television in the old days when Fritz was not talking about his family and about raising his sons. Then, I started to remember all the countless numbers of interviews that were shown on the local Dallas television stations when I was young, growing up in the area.

Fritz could always be seen on camera with one or all of his sons during an interview a few days before one of his big, upcoming matches. When his sons were in college and playing football and basketball or running track, he would always come on television on Saturday nights between matches to let his fans out there know how many touchdowns or baskets his sons had made that week, or what track-record had been broken.

When the boys came into the business with their father, the family interviews continued for many years. They always seemed to be the happiest of families. Then a terrible sadness swept over me at the thought of losing five sons and living alone in the place where so many good memories seemed to be all around. No matter where Fritz went on his 150-acre Lake Dallas Ranch, his sons had been there many years earlier, laughing and playing. I do not think I could handle such unthinkable things happening in my life.

CHAPTER 15

It was nearing the end of August, and Fritz was very excited about the upcoming start of pre-season football. For weeks after the stock markets closed each day we turned off the computer and sat down for our daily glass of Scotch. The two of us would then discuss football. We would not just limit ourselves to one particular NFL team; we talked about all the NFL teams and about college and high school teams as well.

Fritz was a huge football fan. On the Sunday morning before pre-season started, we went through the *Dallas Morning News* and searched the Internet to stay in touch with any late trades or early team news. I sometimes got the impression that Fritz would have traded his wrestling career for a chance at a career in professional football, although he would never admit it.

When the day finally came for the season's first Monday-night football game on television, Fritz was like a little kid. All day long football was all he could think about or talk about. Kevin was coming over to watch the game with us that night and Fritz told me he would be bringing something special to show me. When Kevin arrived, he handed his dad a football. Fritz tossed the football over to me and said, "Read the names, Ron."

As I turned the football over and over in my hands, I begin to read the faded names—Vince Lombardi, Bart Star, Boyd Dowler, Jerry Kramer, Chuck Mercein, and Donny Anderson, to mention a few. I looked up at Fritz and Kevin in disbelief. The ball had been signed by the entire Green Bay Packer football team. A faded date that could barely be made out showed December 31, 1967. My mind raced back, trying to remember why that date sounded so familiar. Then Kevin said, "That's the game ball from the Green Bay and Dallas game." Fritz added, "That's right, one of the game balls from the legendary Ice Bowl."

Fritz and I fixed us a glass of Scotch while Kevin went to the icebox for a beer, and the three of us sat down to talk. "The Ice Bowl"—which was played at Lambeau Field in Green Bay, Wisconsin, in front of a record crowd of 50,861—was said to be the coldest NFL football game ever played, with a temperature that hit thirteen degrees below zero before the end of the game.

"Kevin, David, Kerry, and I were at the game that day," Fritz said.

As we waited for the start of the Monday night football game, Fritz told me about the coldest NFL football game on record.

"I had been wrestling in Green Bay on a Saturday night when the new NFL commissioner, Pete Rozelle, came back to the dressing room and introduced himself to me. We sat in my dressing room talking about the good old days of college football and how I had given up my football career. It turned out Pete was a wrestling fan who had seen me play football at SMU. Pete invited me to come out to the football game that Sunday at Lambeau Field for a match-up between the Green Bay Packers and my favorite team, the Dallas Cowboys.

"I told Pete I had three boys who were out of school for the holidays and were all there in Wisconsin with me. 'All three boys are very big Dallas Cowboy fans and would love to come along,' I said. Pete replied, 'Sure, bring them along with you; we can take them down to the dressing room after the game so they can meet the team.'

"On the way back to the motel that night I told Kevin, David and Kerry that I was going to take them to see their first professional football game on Sunday. Kevin was almost twelve, David nine, and Kerry seven, so they were already into football and looking forward to seeing their first pro game.

"On our way to Lambeau Field early Sunday morning I kept telling the boys that we were going to freeze our butts off. I made the suggestion to them that we should all go back to the hotel and catch the game on television, but they would hear none of that. They wanted to see a pro-football game and the Dallas Cowboys.

"Pete Rozelle had left our names at the front gate and the tickets were for seats on the fifty-yard line behind the Dallas Cowboys' bench. The Cowboys had been my favorite pro-ball club since the franchise began back in 1960, so I was pretty excited about the game. As we entered the stadium, rumors were going around that the game might be postponed because of the extreme cold, but the rumors were wrong. The game was sold out and most of the die-hard football fans did not even seem to notice that it was freezing cold and getting colder. The game began with the Cowboys taking the field.

"In those days, NFL teams had strict dress codes. The Cowboys did not allow players to wear gloves. The Packers did not allow players to wear long underwear that stretched beyond their elbows and knees because it would limit their range of motion.

"On the sidelines, some of the players had their feet wrapped in Saran Wrap. Others wore plastic garbage bags as shirts. As the day went on, it got colder and colder. The wind was blowing so hard that I had thoughts of telling the boys it was time to go home. But they were having a great time and those three boys could care less how cold it was. As it turned out, it was the best damn football game I have ever seen 'til this day.

"At half-time, I had to get up from my frozen seat and walk around some to get the feeling back in my legs. I told the boys to stay in their seats while I went down to the field to talk with some members of the camera crew that I knew from the wrestling arena. While I was talking to some of the guys, I met Steve Sabol, the president of NFL films, which at that time was in its infancy. I had seen Steve running along the sidelines trying to follow the plays on the frozen fields.

"'We hope to make our mark in this game,' Pete had said. But then he told me he was not sure the cameras would make it 'til the end of the game, and as it turned out, seven of the twelve cameras failed that day because the zoom mechanisms froze.

"Sabol said his crew also had debuted boom microphones on that cold day. The boom microphones were round, padded microphones that were hung at the end of a long pole so conversations could be captured from a distance. Pete said he had overheard some of the crew saying that the players thought they were heaters and would grab them to try to get warm. As you can imagine, grabbing the microphones did not do much for sound clarity.

"The Packers won the game 21-17 that very cold day and captured their unprecedented third-straight NFL title. After the game, Pete Rozelle sent someone down to take the boys and me to the locker rooms to meet the teams. He introduced us to the winning team and then gave my boys that game-ball signed by the entire Green Bay Packers football team. After that, we got to go over to the Cowboys dressing room and meet some of our home town players."

Kevin then spoke up and said, "You might notice that the names on the ball are all faded pretty bad. That's because me, Dave, and Kerry played football with it for years before we had enough sense to put it up. When we were young, we never thought about it being valuable someday. David and I just always thought that it was cool that we were playing with the same football that Bart Star played with."

That night, as Fritz, Kevin, and I were watching Monday Night Football and getting somewhat drunk, Kevin started telling a few stories from when he was growing up and starting out in wrestling:

"One time, not long after Dave and I started wrestling as a tag team, one of the top representatives from the Mattel Toy Company got in touch with us after a match one night. We were starting to make a name for ourselves and he wanted to see if we were interested in letting Mattel start making these doll-like action figures of Dave and I, and even one of Dad if he liked the idea. The action figures would be sold at wrestling matches and later in all the toy stores with a large ad campaign on nationwide TV.

"They were cute little dolls with moveable heads, arms, and legs, and their right hands naturally were shaped into the Iron Claw. The Mattel people had even decided the dolls would be called 'World Class Championship Wrestling Action Figures.'

"You have to keep in mind now that they had not yet came out with any type of these action figures; we would have been the first. The Mattel representative had made several in-depth blueprints and drawings that he seemed to be very proud of and wanted to show all of us, while discussing a possible deal. He asked to schedule a meeting with Dave, Dad, and I.

"Dave was the one to schedule the meeting. He made it for 3:30 p.m. at our ranch house on Lake Dallas because that was the only way to get all three of us together in one spot. Because of car problems, though, Dave and I did not get to the house until ten after four that day and we felt very relieved to see that the guy had not arrived yet.

"When we walked in the front door that afternoon, we could smell dinner cooking. We looked at each other and remembered about the same time that we had forgotten to tell Mom about our meeting. We also had not had a chance to explain all the details to Dad, who was just pulling into the driveway. Dave had spoken with Dad earlier that day on the telephone to let him know that we had a business deal we wanted him to sit in on. Dad did not have time to discuss the details with Dave on the phone so he said we would have to talk later. So, as Dad walked into the house, he really did not know what this guy wanted and how much money we all stood to make if the deal went through. Dad was having business problems that day and was not in a very good mood when he arrived home. In addition, he had run over one of Mike's toys that had been left in the driveway, and that put him in an even worse mood.

"Before we had a chance to talk to Dad, Mom ushered all of us into the dining room and decided that she was going to get supper over with as soon as possible because she had made plans for that evening after we all finished eating. Dad loved chili and was just sitting down at the dining room table for a big bowl. Well, it was a standing rule in our house that once supper started, all business and sports talk stopped and did not resume until after everyone had gotten up from the table. After Dave and I decided the guy was not going to show up, we sat down at the table to eat.

"The family had just started passing around the food when the doorbell rang. Both Dave and I jumped up to get the door because this was going to be our first big money deal. Just then, Dad stood up and told Dave and I to sit down and finish eating, that he would handle the person at the door who dared to stand between him and his bowl of chili. The two of us just sat there looking at each other, wanting to say something, but we sat down just the same.

"Dad got up and went to answer the door, as we heard the front door open and Dad's deep voice bellow out, 'What do you want?'

"Dave and I held our breath as we strained our ears to hear what was being said, but we could not make out the words. A little later, Dad came back to the table sat down, and started eating his bowl of chili as if nothing had happened. Dave and I looked at one another, then at Dad, waiting for him to tell us who was at the door, but he said nothing and continued eating.

"Finally, Dave got up enough courage to ask Dad who was at the front door. Dad looked up at us and said, 'It was some guy trying to sell dolls.' I thought Dave was going to choke on his food. 'Dad,' he said, 'that guy represented one of the largest toy manufacturers in the world; they want to make action figures that look like us, not sell us anything. What did you tell him?' David asked.

"Dad looked up again and said, 'I told him that we were eating supper and to come back some other time. I also told the dumbass that we were wrestlers and there were no little girls in our house and we did not need any damn dolls.'

"Dave looked at me and said, 'Well, there went a million dollars apiece.' We sat back down and went on eating. The guy never came back or tried to make another appointment with us. I think that it was less than two years later the WWF action figures hit the market and sold millions."

Several years later, Kerry had an action figure made of him while he was wrestling with the WWF as the Texas Tornado. Fritz said that he still got a small royalty check on Kerry's action figure. The money went into a trust fund for Kerry's two daughters.

"If my two sons had only explained to me what was going on that day and what the hell that guy was talking about, I would not have run him off," Fritz said.

I asked Fritz why Kerry started wrestling for the WWF. He told me it was because Kerry was very self-conscious over the loss of his foot in the motorcycle accident. He was afraid that too many fans in Texas were aware of the accident and the loss of his foot and would not take him seriously in the ring as a contender for the world belt.

"He tried so hard to overcome the loss of that foot and to keep it as much a secret as he could," Kevin said. Then he continued, "I am not too sure that the WWF ever knew that Kerry had a handicap when he first started wrestling for them," Kevin said. "However, a few months after Kerry started working for the WWF, he called me one day and asked if I would come to Atlanta and be his tag team partner. I said sure, and caught the next flight to Atlanta. After the family had tried to talk Kerry into giving up wrestling, he had left town and we did not know where he was until he called me that day. That was one of the reasons I decided to go to Atlanta and tag with him.

"I wrestled with the WWF off and on for a while trying to keep an eye on Kerry, but I had a wife and four children in Texas and did not like to stay away from home that much. I knew he was having a lot of pain, especially after the matches were over. Sometimes he would be in so much pain that I would have to help him get back to the dressing room. It seemed like every time I saw him he was taking a handful of pain medicine. He took them before every match and after every match. I just did not know what to do or say about it.

"One night, Kerry and I were in a tag team match in New York City at Madison Square Gardens," Kevin said. "Kerry was in the ring, being ganged up on in the opponent's corner, and I jumped into the ring to help him. The referee escorted me back to my corner, telling me only two men were allowed in the ring at one time. When I got back to my corner and turned around, Kerry was gone and the referee and our opponents were looking all around for him. I thought I heard someone call out my name, so I jumped off the ring and onto the floor. And there was Kerry, hiding under the ring apron. He had lost his prosthetic foot.

"'Kevin,' he screamed. 'I lost my foot! You have to go find it for me.'

"What?" I asked. "You lost your foot? Well, where did you lose it?

"'Over in the other corner,' said Kerry.

"With everyone looking at me as if I had totally lost my mind, I walked over to the other corner where Kerry's foot was just lying on the floor. I picked it up and took it back to him; Kerry reached out from under the ring and grabbed it out of my hand. The fans around ringside looked at me with their mouths hanging open, not knowing what had just happened. All the fans at ringside did not know Kerry had a prosthetic foot, so it just looked like I was handing him his boot, but I think some of the fans must have thought that Kerry's foot was still in his boot because of the looks on their faces. Kerry and I laughed so hard after the match was over that my side hurt."

As the night went on, Kevin, Fritz, and I talked about the WWF and wrestling today. Fritz said the World Wrestling Federation was started back in 1963 by Vincent J. McMahon Sr., who had been a longtime promoter in the Northeast."

Vince Sr. and I had been friends for many years before he started the WWF. After about a year, Vince Sr. left the National Wrestling Alliance (NWA). He and longtime friend Joseph 'Toots' Mondt started to promote shows independent from the NWA under the name World Wide Wrestling Federation (WWWF). The story was given to the fans that the promoters had disputed a decision in the Lou Thesz and Buddy Rogers World Championship match, so in late 1963, Buddy Rogers was recognized as the WWWF World Heavyweight Champion.

"It was around 1970 that Vince K. McMahon, Vince Sr.'s son, started working in professional wrestling as a broadcaster. I was president of the National Wrestling Alliance and Vince Sr. and I worked very closely with one another. By about 1972, wrestling attendance had started dropping off in many states so Vince Sr. and I sat down and came up with a plan to bring pro-wrestling back if attendance continued to fall. We never implemented that plan, but kept it as a back-up just in case. A couple of years later, Vince Sr. decided to get out of the business due to health problems. In 1979, the WWWF changed its name back to the World Wrestling Federation, as it is known today.

"In about the middle of 1982, Vince Jr. purchased Capitol Wrestling Corp. (the legal entity of the WWF) from his father and formed Titan Sports as the parent company of the promotion. It was then that Vince Jr. implemented the plan that his father and I had come up with years earlier. That plan would change the way the wrestling business was run from then on.

"Vince Jr. has done a very good job making the wrestling business what it is today. He took a great idea, put his own personal touch to it, and came out a winner.

"A funny story that I heard a few years back occurred when Ted Turner of Turner Broadcasting bought out the NWA. He called Vince Jr. on the phone one day and said, 'Hey Vince, guess what?' And Vince said, 'I give up, Ted, what?' Ted then replied, 'I just bought out The National Wrestling Alliance, so I guess I am now in the wrestling business, too.' After a long pause, Vince Jr. said, 'That's great, Ted, but I am in the entertainment business,' and he hung up the phone.

"This is one of the reasons why I have always felt that Vince Jr. would take the WWF a long way. He knows what business he is in. Please do not get me wrong, the injuries are just as real and these boys in today's wrestling put their lives and careers on the line to bring the fans high-risk moves never before seen in the wrestling business, but it is still very different from the wrestling of my day.

"The one thing that I have noticed about the wrestling business after all these years is that the pro wrestling fan is not a dying breed. Professional wrestling still packs arenas all over the world, and I think it will continue to do so for many years to come.

"I remember a time when a ticket to a wrestling match cost about twenty-five cents and would give you around three hours of entertainment. The only overhead that the promoter had was the cost of the arena and the wrestlers' salaries. Now you cannot get in the door for much less than twenty dollars, and you're lucky if you can get two hours of entertainment, and promoters' overhead is hundreds of thousands of dollars per show. It is a very big business and getting bigger as the years pass, not just in our country, but also in countries all over the world."

CHAPTER 16

As the summer days passed by, chemotherapy began to take its toll on Fritz's body as he grew weaker and weaker. His hair was starting to fall out, so one day he asked me to shave his head. I shaved off what was left of Fritz's hair, then handed him a mirror. Fritz looked up at me and said he needed a glass of Scotch to help him work up the courage to look at himself in the mirror.

I obliged and poured us both a glass of Scotch. After we had finished our first drink, I poured us each a second glass of Scotch and then handed Fritz the mirror for a second time. He studied his image in the reflection for a very long moment, then started laughing aloud, saying he thought he looked like George "The Animal" Steele, except with glasses.

"The Animal" was an older wrestler from the sixties, seventies, and eighties whose real name was James Meyers. He had no hair on his head and he always painted his tongue green when he wrestled. He would come out of the dressing room on his way to the ring, acting like some kind of a maniac. Then, when he got to the ring, he would start banging his head on the turnbuckle and foaming a green substance from the mouth. At times, George was even known to rip into the turnbuckle with his teeth, tearing off a piece of the leather to eat for the benefit of the audience.

"I shouldn't have said that about old George," said Fritz. "He's really a hell of a nice guy. He worked for the WCCW on a few occasions in Dallas and always drew large crowds. Wrestling fans seem to love coming to the matches to see the crazy, insane type of wrestler, and George sure fit into that category."

James Meyers was born in 1937 in Detroit and started his wrestling career there in the early sixties. Before that, George was a schoolteacher in Detroit. He had first started out wearing a mask and wrestled as "The Student," with "Playboy" Gary Hart as his manager. He later dropped the mask and became George "The Animal" Steele. From the beginning, George was known as a wild-man who could not be controlled. He wrestled in the Detroit area for years, earning the name "The Detroit Madman." Referee Al Vass once said, "Trying to referee a George Steele match was like being trapped in a steel cage with a rabid Saint Bernard."

By the last week in August, Fritz had become so weak that he had trouble standing up by himself. On several occasions he fell down and could not get back up without help. Unfortunately, I had undergone lower back surgery a couple of years earlier and could not lift his 265 pounds off the floor by myself. When he fell, I would have to call Kevin to come and help him up off the ground.

One evening, while Fritz and I were outside working in his pepper garden, Fritz fell down and could not get back up. As hard as I tried, I could not pull him up by myself. I walked back up to the house to use the phone and call Kevin, but Kevin was not home. So I headed back outside to tell Fritz that we had this major problem. As I walked up to Fritz, I noticed that he was lying on his back looking at two birds in a tree beside him. "Fritz," I said, "we have a big problem."

"Ron, don't you dare tell me that Kevin is not at home," he said.

"Okay, Fritz," I replied. "I will not tell you that Kevin is not home; I will just tell you it will be a few hours before he can get here."

"Damn, Ron. You have to get me off the ground; I feel like a dumbass. Besides, with all the cars driving by the house and you standing over my body with that stupid look on your face, people will think you just killed me."

"Good," I replied. "Maybe one of them will stop and help me get you off the ground."

I suggested to Fritz that I just go back up to the house and call 911 and see if they would send someone out to his house to help. At this Fritz began cussing me, saying he could just see the headlines in tomorrow's Denton newspaper: "Fritz Von Erich Has Fallen and He Cannot Get Back Up."

At this, we each laughed and lit a cigarette as I tried to figure out a way to get Fritz up on his feet. After a few minutes, Fritz came up with a plan. I was to go back to the house and get the pickup truck and find a long piece of rope. We could then tie the rope onto the bumper of the pickup and Fritz could hold onto the other end. Then, I would pull slowly forward while he dug his feet in the ground and let the truck pull him up.

Therefore, I went back to the house and looked around until I found a piece of rope long enough to do the job. I climbed into the truck and started driving to where Fritz lay on the ground. I, too, could imagine the headlines in tomorrow's Denton newspaper: "Man Charged in the Dragging Death of Fritz Von Erich."

The first attempt did not go as well as we had planned. Fritz turned to his left a little too much and fell back to the ground after almost making it to his feet. I got out of the truck and asked him if he wanted me to call 911 yet. He gave me a go-to-hell look, called me a few names, and told me to get back in the truck and try again. "I think I have the hang of it now," he said. On the second try, the truck pulled him to his feet.

As I got out of the truck I noticed the look of pain on Fritz's face. "Are you all right?" I asked.

"Yes, I am fine," Fritz said. "But I think we're going to have to hit the Scotch early tonight. I hurt all over."

The doctors at the hospital had tried to talk Fritz into taking pain medication, but he always refused, saying Scotch and pot were all he needed. Nonetheless, the doctors sent Kevin home with a bottle of liquid morphine sulfate one day, just in case the pain got too bad for Fritz to handle. That day could be right around the corner, the doctors had said.

I spent four years in the United States Marine Corp and two years as a police officer. As a rifleman in Vietnam and a cop in Seattle, Washington, I had seen men shot, stabbed, and injured in every way a person could imagine. The pain I watched some men go through haunts me to this very day. Nevertheless, I must say that I have never in my life seen a man with such a high pain threshold as Fritz Von Erich. There were many times when I could see the pain in his eyes but he would never let out a sound or complain about how bad he felt. To him, pain was something he had lived with all his life, so he refused to give in to it now that he was sick and nearing the end of his life.

September had arrived and Fritz began asking the doctors if they thought he would live to see the Super Bowl. By this time, football had become so important in Fritz's life it seemed to be the only thing he looked forward to. He and I would start off our weekends by watching all the college football games each Saturday. Then, when Sunday came, it was the NFL all day long. Fritz even had me set up a second small television next to his larger one; both televisions had picture-in-a-picture so we could watch four games at the same time.

It was Monday, September 8. The weekend had gone like so many others, with Fritz and me sitting in front of the television watching one football game after the other. Kevin was coming over to watch Monday Night Football with us and I was planning to cook steaks on the grill. Kevin had not been over to see his dad in almost a week due to several arguments the two of them were having concerning Fritz's Last Will and Testament. I was woken up early one morning by Fritz screaming at Kevin in the kitchen, saying, "DAMN YOU KEVIN, YOU SCREW THAT BOY OVER AND I WILL COME BACK FROM THE DEAD AND HAUNT YOU FOR THE REST OF YOUR LIFE." Later that day, Fritz told me that one of his and Kevin's arguments that morning had concerned me. Fritz had told Kevin that he wanted for me to be able to live in his small frame house on the 150 acres for as long as I wanted for all the help I had given him over the past several months, and Kevin had not agreed.

"Ron, I would like to be able to do something for you before I die. I know Kevin; he's a very greedy person and will screw you over when I'm dead and out of the picture, so please let me do something for you." I thanked Fritz for his concern, but told him that I had a house in Irving and I would be fine. "Okay!" he said. "If you won't live in my house, then let me buy you a new pick-up truck." I again refused, saying that if he bought me a new truck it would cause problems between me and Kevin and for him not to worry about me, that I would make it just fine. "Ron, you're a one-of-a-kind person," he said, "and I guess that the only thing I can do for you is thank you from the bottom of my heart for all the help you have given me. And when my life is over, and if it turns out that there is a God and I make to heaven, I will certainly tell him to keep a special eye on you."

"Thanks, Fritz," I said. "That means more to me than anything you could buy me."

When Kevin arrived that evening, he brought some wine to go with our steaks, but Fritz did not eat or drink. He said he was not hungry and that he would try to eat something later. By half-time, Fritz had hardly said a word since Kevin arrived. I looked over at him, and he was sitting at the kitchen table with his head down. I told Kevin that I did not think his father was feeling well.

"Dad, are you all right?" Kevin asked. Fritz raised his head. "I think something is bad wrong, Kevin," Fritz said. "My insides hurt bad and my head feels strange."

Kevin's wife Pam had come over and the three of us tried to get Fritz to go to bed, but he insisted on sitting at the kitchen table and watching the rest of the game. He later told me he was afraid that if he went to bed and fell asleep he would never wake up.

As time passed by that night, Fritz got worse. He was moaning aloud and fading in and out of consciousness. At one point he lifted his head and looked me right in the eyes and screamed, "Goddamn it, Ron, do something!"

I shook my head, and with a tear in my eye I said, "I am sorry, Fritz, but I just do not know what I can do."

I turned around and told Kevin that we should give him an eyedropper of the morphine sulfate and see if that would help, since Fritz was still moaning as if in lots of pain. After I gave Fritz the morphine, he seemed to calm down somewhat and was trying to talk. Kevin then stepped over to the kitchen cabinets and poured a glass of Scotch and said, "Here, Dad, drink this." I stopped Kevin, saying not to let him drink alcohol while I was giving him the morphine.

The football game was over and it had started getting late as Kevin and I sat at the kitchen table watching Fritz. He was still fading in and out of consciousness and would start swatting the air with his hand as if trying to get something out of his face. About five hours had passed since I had last given Fritz an eyedropper full of the morphine and he had started moaning aloud again; I told Kevin that I was going to give his dad another dose. After another eyedropper full of morphine, Fritz started calming down and I got up from the table to go to the restroom. As I returned, I noticed Kevin standing over his dad with the bottle of morphine and the eyedropper in his hand. I yelled at Kevin, telling him that I had just given Fritz some morphine and if he gave him any more it could kill him.

Kevin said, "Oh! Okay, I did not see you give him any." I just stared at Kevin for a moment, knowing that he had just watched me give his dad an eyedropper full of the morphine sulfate. Kevin then put the lid back on the morphine, sat it back on the kitchen table, and walked into another room. I walked over to the table where Fritz sat and picked up the bottle of morphine to examine it. It seemed to me that some of the morphine was missing, but I could not be sure and did not want to believe what I thought that I had just witnessed.

As I turned to go into the other room, I planned to ask Kevin if he had given his dad more morphine when Kevin and Pam came walking out toward the back door, saying that they had decided to go back to their house and were going to call the hospice nurse and ask if there was anything else that could be done. It was a few hours later when the nurse finally called. The nurse asked me how much morphine we had given Fritz; I told her that I had given him two eyedroppers-full and was not sure what Kevin had given him. She then said not to give him any more by mouth and for me to get the nebulizer out; then she told me how to use it. The nebulizer was a device with a facemask that would heat the morphine into a mist that I could use to spray the medicine directly into Fritz's nose or mouth.

I explained to the nurse that Fritz was sitting at the dining room table, unconscious, and that I could not get him in bed by myself. She told me to do the best I could until she could get there and that she would have a hospital bed brought to us in a few hours.

I spent the rest of morning sitting at the table with Fritz. Every few minutes he would start moving around in his chair and moaning. I did not want to use the nebulizer since I was unsure of how much morphine he had actually been given, knowing from my experiences in Vietnam that too much morphine sulfate could induce a comma. At one point Fritz started moving around in his chair so much I was afraid he might fall on the floor, but he settled down after I began talking to him for a few minutes and assuring him that I was by his side and would not leave him. I started telling Fritz about how I grew up watching him wrestle and how much he had impacted my life, and at one point I think I saw him smile at me.

At about 10:30 Tuesday morning, Pam called to ask how Fritz was doing and to say that she and Kevin were on their way over. The nurse showed up a little after eleven o'clock that morning and Fritz's bed was delivered around noon. It took everyone in the house to get him from the dining room table to the hospital bed, which had been set up in the living room.

The nurse noticed how tired I looked and suggested I get some sleep. So many people were starting to show up to see how Fritz was doing that I decided it would be best if I went on home to Irving. When I got to my house I was so tired I went right to bed, but I could not sleep. I was worried about the man I had spent the last three months taking care of and getting to know so well, knowing deep down inside that I would not see him alive again. After tossing and turning for about an hour, I finally got up, went out, and grabbed a hamburger, took two muscle relaxers that had been prescribed for my back and went back to bed.

I had been so tired that it was around eleven o'clock Wednesday morning when I finally open my eyes. I went right to the phone to call Kevin's house. There was no answer, so I tried Fritz's home phone number and got a busy signal. I jumped in the shower, got dressed, and headed back to Lake Dallas. When I arrived at Fritz's house, Kevin saw me pull up and came out to the truck. He told me they had just pronounced his dad dead.

Fritz had never regained consciousness after I left Tuesday morning. I expressed my sympathies to Kevin and his family and told him I was going into the house to see my friend and longtime hero one last time. After I said my goodbyes to Fritz, I got in the truck and headed back to my house in Irving. On the way I stopped at the liquor store and bought a bottle of Scotch. When I arrived back at my house, I sat down and got very drunk.

That night I cried for the first time in many years. After getting through Vietnam by the skin of my teeth and losing so many friends over there, I thought I was immune to the feeling that death left behind. However, I was wrong.

Fritz had a very nice memorial service. There were many friends and fans in attendance and Kevin said a few last words to thank all the fans for their support, phone calls, and get-well cards. After the service, Fritz's body was immediately cremated and his ashes were buried at the head of Kerry's grave. There was no funeral or graveside service. The next day, the *Dallas Morning News* ran a long article about Fritz.

******

News articles were taken from the *Dallas Morning News* archives: all articles are printed as they appeared.

VON ERICH WRESTLING PATRIARCH DIES Jack Adkisson, 68, built name and empire but suffered tragic loss of 5 sons

By: Kevin Sherrington/staff writer of the *Dallas Morning News*
Published, September 11, 1997

Jack Adkisson, patriarch of professional wrestling's famous and tragic Von Erich family, died at his Lake Dallas home Wednesday of complications from cancer. He was 68.

Mr. Adkisson, who used the stage name Fritz Von Erich, outlived five sons. The oldest, Jack Jr., died in a 1959 accident at the age of 6. David, the first to follow his father into wrestling, died of an intestinal illness in 1984 at 24.

But three other sons—Mike, Chris and Kerry, who all wrestled under the Von Erich name—took their own lives between 1987 and 1993.

Only Kevin, age 40, remains.

"Like any of us, he hurt tremendously for those losses," said Marc Lawrence, host of one of Mr. Adkisson's wrestling shows from 1980 through 1990. "He had a tremendous amount of questions as to why. But he knew that someday those mysteries would be solved. Perhaps today is that day." Doctors first discovered a cancerous tumor in one of Mr. Adkisson's lungs when he was admitted to Baylor Medical Center on July 25 after a mild stroke.

Six weeks ago, they discovered that the cancer had spread to his brain.

"We would like to express thanks to the fans and community for their prayers, love and support," Kevin Adkisson said in a news release. "Dad loved them very much."

Jack Adkisson grew up in East Dallas and attended old Crozier Tech. He lettered in football at Southern Methodist University in 1949 and was a member of the first Dallas Texans football team in the early 1950s. His blond hair worn in a crew cut, he pretended to be a Nazi sympathizer at matches. He played to the jeers as he goose stepped into the ring, his 6-foot-4, 260-pound frame an imposing presence. The "iron claw"—a wrestling hold that reputedly rendered opponents helpless—was his signature move.

By the end of his wrestling days, however, he had switched from villain to hero. The role better suited his private life in later years, when he spoke at Evangelical Christian meetings, as did his sons.

He retired in 1985 with a match in Texas Stadium against King Kong Bundy. By that time, Mr. Adkisson was producing a syndicated wrestling show called World Class Championship Wrestling that ran in 66 national television markets as well as Japan, Argentina and the Middle East. Until the late 1980s, he ran wrestling at the Sportatorium, the aging relic on the southwest fringe of downtown Dallas.

In 1987, KXTX-TV (Channel 39) paid him $226,752 for the television rights to World Class Championship Wrestling.

"He was a man who revolutionized wrestling on TV," said Mr. Lowrance, now a Methodist pastor outside Fort Worth. "He was the first to have his own wrestling card seen in everyone else's market."

Rene Valadez, 38, and Carol Herrera, 36, both of San Antonio, said they became wrestling fans while watching Mr. Adkisson's productions on television in South Texas.

"He was fantastic in his own right," Ms. Herrera said. "He was the ultimate of wrestlers. He was booed, but he was still respected."

But Mr. Adkisson's lasting fame would come from his family, not as a solo act. "When you think of Texas wrestling," Ms. Valadez said, "you think of the first family of wrestling."

"Which is the Von Erichs," Ms. Herrera said.

David was the first to follow his father's fame. At 6-foot-7, with red hair and blue eyes, David was the most charismatic, wrestling observers say. He collapsed while on a 1984 tour in Japan and died of enteritis, an inflammation of the intestines.

Problems soon mounted for the other brothers. Mike nearly died in 1985 when he contracted toxic shock syndrome after shoulder surgery. Family members considered his recovery a miracle. But Mike, 23, took an overdose of sleeping pills in 1987. He left a note that read,

"Dear Mom, you've always been wonderful. I am in a better place, and David and I will be watching."

His mother, Doris Adkisson, would suffer through the deaths of two more children over the next six years. The youngest, Chris, who never matched up physically with his brothers, killed himself in 1991 with a gunshot wound in the head. He was 21. Two years later, 33-year-old Kerry, on probation and about to be arrested on a cocaine charge, also shot himself.

"The thing about Fritz was that he was very domineering, both as an employer and a father," said Stan Hovatter Jr., who worked for Mr. Adkisson as a publicist in the mid-1980s. "There was no question he loved his kids, and he was trying to build them an empire they could take over and run. But what Fritz didn't really understand was that not all the boys wanted to wrestle."

Nevertheless, their popularity was unprecedented in local circles. At an autograph session in 1987 at Town East mall, "fans made a mess of the place," Mr. Hovatter said. "Even then, they were the thing of wrestling."

"I had no idea it was going to skyrocket," Mrs. Adkisson once said of her sons' popularity in the early 1980s. "It was like riding a shooting star. You have no idea when it will stop. But it will stop."

The deaths hastened it. The family lived under that pall for more than 40 years. It started when Jack Jr. died when he touched an exposed power line at the family home in 1959.

Mrs. Adkisson told the *Dallas Morning News* in 1993 that the death of each of her sons only added to her initial pain. "I'm in different stages for each one," she said. "I still grieve for my 6-year-old. None of them you get over." Mrs. Adkisson, who divorced her husband in 1992 after 42 years of marriage, was not available for comment Wednesday.

She told the *Dallas Morning News* in 1993 that somehow a "seed" of suicide was planted in her son's head. A few months after Mike's death in 1987, the parents told another News reporter that the memories of their children as boys sustained them.

"We've always believed that the best times are when you're doing something special with your kids," Mr. Adkisson said. "Doris and I used to watch them in little track meets. People would say, 'Your boys sure are lucky to have you here to watch them.' Heck, Doris and I felt we were the lucky ones."

His life did not always bear witness to that. But he never allowed it to overcome him, friends said. "He was big, he was gruff, and he had a very keen sense of humor," Mr. Lowrance said.

"I think he was deeply compassionate. Those of us who worked with him were part of his extended family."

A memorial service will be held at noon Saturday at the First Baptist Church of Dallas. Dr. Criswell and Dr. O.S. Hawkins will officiate.

Family members say there will be no funeral or graveside services. Mr. Adkisson will be buried at Grove Hill Memorial Park in East Dallas, next to his sons.

One last thing that I would like to share with you: Three days after Fritz passed away, an article appeared in the *Dallas Morning News* about the famed Southside Sportatorium. Here are a couple of paragraphs from that news article.

DALLAS DIARY
Time catches up with fabled Sportatorium

Published, September 14, 1997

For more than a half a century, the Sportatorium has provided a wrestling venue for the likes of Black Bart, Mad Mike Mazurki, Duke Keomuka, and the world famous Von Erich family.

And when matches weren't scheduled, famous stars such as Elvis Presley and Willy Nelson performed in the huge metal barn of a building.

Sadly, the Sportatorium's colorful history ends tonight. The last wrestling events will be held this evening. The building's new owners are talking about tearing it down and putting a convenience store and gas station on the site.

What a loss. Dallas will never have another place like the Sportatorium. In these days of vanishing innocence, there may never be a place where good and evil are so clearly defined. Its passing deserves a wake.

Fritz and his family helped with so many charitable organizations throughout the United States and Texas, especially in the way of donations for child-related illnesses that a sculpture of Fritz's right hand in the shape of his devastating Iron Claw can be seen on display in the lobby of Children's Hospital in Dallas, Texas.

I will remember the time that I spent with the late Fritz Von Erich for the rest of my life. It has been almost seven years since Fritz passed away. Kevin and I are no longer friends and have not spoken to each other since shortly after Fritz's death. I have tried to put this book out of my mind because of not having enough faith in myself and not knowing what I should say and should not say. I started and stopped this book several different times before getting serious. However, the promise that I made before Fritz died has always remained strong.

For a couple of years, I sat down every now and then and tried to write something that made sense, but the words just never came. Then, one morning, at around 3:25 a.m., I awoke from a dream about Fritz and myself. In my dream, Fritz and I were taking our morning walk around Fritz's ranch on Lake Dallas, which was what we usually did when I stayed with him before he passed away. Fritz was telling me in my dream that it was time for me to write the book about his life that we had talked so much about.

I remember telling Fritz in my dream that I could not think of the words to say and that everything I put down on paper never came out sounding the way I wanted. At this, his voice rang out so loudly that I woke up. "Ron," Fritz said, "you took good notes like I told you to, you stayed with me until the very end, and you know my story. Now sit down and just put the notes together. If you will just try, it will all come to you."

I got out of bed that morning, washed my face, sat down at my computer, and started to write the story just as Fritz had told it to me. And just as Fritz had told me in my dream, the words seem to come from nowhere. Because I feel in my heart that Fritz himself guided me though the many times that I almost gave up on a promise I made to him years earlier.

"Fritz Von Erich" should have been remembered as a giant in the history of professional wrestling.

Instead, his name is synonymous with the tragedy and grief that the sport of professional wrestling—or any other full-contact sport—can sometimes cause.

Printed in the USA
CPSIA information can be obtained
at www.ICGtesting.com
LVHW040349290224
772928LV00003B/413

9 781635 249811